D1356097

Mad, Bad and Dangerous To Know

*Reflections of a
Forensic Practitioner*

Herschel Prins

Mad, Bad and Dangerous To Know

*Reflections of a
Forensic Practitioner*

Herschel Prins

WATERSIDE PRESS

Mad, Bad and Dangerous to Know
Reflections of a Forensic Practitioner
Herschel Prins

Published 2010 by
Waterside Press Ltd.
Sherfield Gables
Sherfield on Loddon
Hook, Hampshire
United Kingdon RG27 0JG

Telephone +44(0)1256 882250 Low cost UK landline calls 0845 2300 733
E-mail enquiries@watersidepress.co.uk **Online catalogue** WatersidePress.co.uk

ISBN 9781904380 580 (Hardback)

Cataloguing-In-Publication Data A catalogue record for this book can be
obtained from the British Library.

Cover design © 2010 Waterside Press.

UK distributor Gardners Books, 1 Whittle Drive, Eastbourne, East Sussex,
BN23 6QH. Tel: +44 (0)1323 521777; sales@gardners.com; gardners.com

North American distributor International Specialised Book Services (ISBS),
920 NE 58th Ave, Suite 300, Portland, Oregon, 97213-3786, USA
Tel: 1 800 944 6190 Fax 1 503 280 8832 orders@isbs.com www.isbs.com

e-book *Mad, Bad and Dangerous to Know* is available as an ebook (e-book
ISBN 9781906534837) and also to subscribers of Myilibrary and Dawsonera.

Printed in Great Britain by the MPG Books Group, Bodmin and King's Lynn

Contents

'Herschel Prins' lifelong commitment to a deeper understanding of offending behaviour as practitioner, academic and author is remarkable. His work reflects a warm and generous spirit allied to a rigorous method and a shrewd intellect. In a field prone to disappointment and disillusion he continues to stimulate and inspire': **Sir Michael Day OBE**

'Herschel Prins was not just a pioneer in psychiatric social work but one of the first people to recognise the need for multi-disc-plinary work between psychiatrists, psychologists, the courts, lawyers, social workers, probation officers and others. As a leading scholar of his generation focusing on forensic work with offenders, dangerous or otherwise, I can think of no-one more instrumental at the pivotal meeting point of crime, criminal justice and mental disorder': **Andrew Rutherford**

'On the tomb of Sir Christopher Wren in St Paul's Cathedral, the visitor will read the inscription, *Si monumentum requiris, circum-spice* (If you are wanting a monument, just look around you). In the field of mental health - as probation inspector, forensic practi-tioner, psychiatric social worker, criminologist, teacher in criminal justice, inquisitor in public inquiries and author - Herschel Prins' career has been marked by a monument to unassertive sanity': **Sir Louis Blom-Cooper QC**

Every act of authority of one man over another, for which there is not
an absolute necessity, is tyrannical.
Cesare Becarria, *Dei Delitti e Delle Pene* (1776)

It is the very error of the moon; she comes more near the earth
than she was wont and makes men mad.
Othello, Act V, Sc.ii

O! Let me not be mad, not that sweet heaven; keep me in
temper; I would not be mad!
King Lear, Act I, Sc.v)

Canst thou not minister to a mind diseas'd?
Macbeth, Act V, Sc.iii

Mad, Bad and Dangerous to know.
Caroline Lamb describing Byron, 1812

If a man will begin with certainties, he shall end in doubts;
but if he will be content to begin with doubts
he shall end in certainties.
Francis Bacon, 1st Baron Verulam and Viscount St. Albans,
The Advancement of Learning (1605)

Foreword

I can't now remember when I first met the author of this book, but long before I did I was already very aware of his work as one of - if not the - key figure in Britain who had pushed forward the development of criminology and forensic psychiatry. It may have been at an Editorial Board meeting of the *Howard Journal of Criminal Justice* in the 1980s – at that time held in Doughty Street, where Dickens had once lived, and when I was still an Assistant Prison Governor. Or, perhaps it was through a conference organised by Nacro (which at that time was still proud to spell out each of the letters of its name, and before it decided to bid to run prisons) and for whom Herschel chaired the Committee on Mentally Disordered Offenders, and at which he seemed to spend his time persisting – never demanding – that society should improve their treatment of the mentally ill. I can't remember where, or in what circumstances, but I do remember asking a friend 'Who's that?' and thinking how much I admired this decent and humane man who spoke such good sense and who was called Herschel Prins.

Herschel began his career as a probation officer in 1952, and since that date and role he has worked at the Home Office and as the Director of Social Work at Leicester University. He has held appointments at a number of universities and currently holds professorial posts at Leicester and Loughborough universities. He has also worked on the Parole Board, the Mental Health Act Commission, and the Mental Health Review Tribunal, and a small indicator of the esteem in which he is held amongst mental health professionals can be gauged by the fact that in 2001 when the Glenfield Hospital opened a centre for the treatment of patients who had committed a crime as a result of mental illness they named it The Herschel Prins Low Secure Centre.

He has been a stalwart of the Editorial Board of the *Howard Journal of Criminal Justice* – where I can always rely on him to actually turn up to meetings – and is a member of the board of five other professional or academic journals. In 1999 his academic peers and colleagues published *Mentally Disordered Offenders: Managing People Nobody Owns* edited by David Webb and Robert Harris in tribute to him, and in which they noted his 'humanising and civilizing' work and influence on lawyers, social workers, students, fellow academics, practitioners, and others.

And yet all these awards and distinctions hardly capture a life that has been devoted to arsonists, psychopaths, sexual deviants and those among us who behave bizarrely and dangerously. Herschel has spent his professional life working with the troubled and the troublesome, the unloved (and the often unlovely) where the consistent theme of his work has been to combine the practical with an awareness of what is possible when one works with mentally disordered offenders. Why choose that life and these clients? What demands has that choice made on him, his family, his colleagues?

Mad, Bad and Dangerous to Know (note, no question mark) sets out to answer these – and other – questions. This is no small matter, for while we have all got used to ex-offenders (and to some extent ex-police and prison staff) writing their memoirs there are still very few autobiographies of criminologists that we can turn to so as to uncover the unsteady and heady development of the discipline since the Second World War. As such, *Mad, Bad and Dangerous to Know* will be of interest to a wide range of academics and practitioners and can be read as a blueprint for how to engage policy-makers and the public with an often reviled type of offender.

The approach mentioned in the previous paragraph is now being termed 'public criminology', although Hershel Prins, clearly ahead of his time, got there long before the rest of us.

Some of you reading this Foreword might think that I have gone too far, that I have been over generous, or that Herschel or his publishers have offered me some kind of inducement! Nothing can be further from the truth, and it is simply wonderful for me to be able to pay tribute to one of my heroes, and to put on record my personal admiration for this humble, modest, decent but quite extraordinary man.

Professor David Wilson

Centre of Applied Criminology, Birmingham City University
January 2010

Preface

The main title of this book is, of course, derived from the statement by Lady Caroline Lamb of Byron in her *Journal* of 1812. It requires a little elaboration since I hope very much that the contents of it will appeal not only to professionals in the socio-forensic arena but to the wider public interested in furthering their knowledge through the 'lens' of someone who has had to confront the activities of the mad and the bad through five and a half decades of work 'in the field'.

Possibly and maybe ideally, I should have added a question mark after the title - and readers may in turn ask why. The answer is at one and the same time both simple and complex; for an individual can be mad and bad and sometimes mad or bad. And when does mere eccentricity shade into madness? I have met many eccentric colleagues in my working life; I have sometimes thought them to be not a little mad. And at times, I have behaved with eccentricity myself, perhaps to the point of madness.

Such distinctions often pose forensic problems. Many years ago, a very respected friend and colleague of mine, a psychiatrist with much experience of dealing with madness and badness said, as I recall,

> Well Herschel, the courts deal with murder cases for example. A few such offenders are clinically mad; others just have nasty habits like killing people!

Alongside such problems of demarcation resides the prognostication of 'dangerousness'. My experience has taught me on more than one occasion that the prognostication is not an exact science. It may well reside in the eye (or sometimes in the stomach) of the beholder. Sometimes these 'organs' will produce a degree of over and under cautiousness and a failure to see what may lie right under one's nose.

I need not dwell on these matters here (I dealt with them at length in various publications, including in the various editions of my book *Offenders, Deviants or Patients?: Explorations in Clinical Criminology.*[1] However, in the vignettes which follow I have tried to bring out the kind of challenges faced every day by practitioners like myself who try to bring what is deemed to be an expert approach to matters which also raise fundamental questions.

The vignettes are composites. Although derived from real cases the scenarios which they depict have been rendered anonymous and their constituent parts (I hope) unidentifiable. Despite these necessary ethical precautions they provide sufficiently authentic accounts of the matters which they are intended to represent.

In the chapters which follow I explain how I came to be involved in this 'mad, bad and dangerous world', the twists and turns of my career, the places to which it took me, some of the things I learned along the way and the people who had an effect on my professional or in some cases personal life. Also part a 'survivors manual' and part collection of forensic language and preoccupations, I hope that those starting out in this field will find it to be of as much interest as more seasoned observers.

Vignette 1: The 'No-hoper'

'William' was labelled as a 'no-hoper' by some people. He was in his late sixties. And, as I discovered more than once, he could

1. (2010) *Offenders, Deviants or Patients: Routledge.* (Edn. 4).

become very abusive, verbally and physically. From time-to-time he would commit what can best be described as public order offences. As a result, he became very well-known to people working in the mental health and criminal justice systems.

William floated like some piece of flotsam upon the waters of both systems, Is he to be deemed 'mad' (in common parlance) because of his alcohol abuse or merely 'bad' because he is such a noisy nuisance? I often had to deal with him because others had given up on him and no-one was prepared to 'own' him. As with many others like him, someone had to.

Vignette 2: The 'Flasher'

'Geoffrey' was a comparatively minor sex offender. He was in his mid-fifties. He had a long history of 'flashing', which is short-hand for indecent exposure. He admitted that he had engaged in such conduct on many more occasions than those for which he had eventually been prosecuted and convicted in court.

Geoffrey had received a wide range of penal and mental health disposals, including numerous periods of probation (as it was then called) combined with psychiatric treatment. Despite the anxiety he used to feel at each court appearance he claimed that he was quite unable to break his compulsive behaviour. Probation officers (such as myself on occasion and at that stage in my career), and mental health professionals had tried various forms of therapy.

Was his compulsion just a highly ingrained habit or should he be labelled 'mentally impaired'? The behaviour of offenders like Geoffrey is highly distressing to many victims (usually young women or children). In some cases it may take a more serious turn and end in a serious sexual crime involving violence (and causing the offender to be deemed 'dangerous'). In such instances the prediction of dangerousness may be an important task and responsibility for the professional. Hence the words 'comparatively minor' used at the start of this vignette. Such terms are commonly bandied about but need to be viewed with caution.

Vignette 3: A More Serious Offender

'Peter' was a more serious repeat sex offender. He was in his late forties and hailed from the West Country. Some decades earlier he had been sent to a high security hospital (in those days known as a special hospital) on an order under the mental health legislation 'restricting his discharge' except in limited circumstances.

Peter had been diagnosed and classified as suffering from psychopathic disorder. He had an extensive criminal record of sexual offending. The victims of his last offence had been 'groomed' by him for some time and were all young boys. After several years in hospital where Peter had received a range of treatments for his sexual deviancy he had been discharged into the community under supervision. He had been at liberty for about four years when he was apprehended for further offences of a similar nature. However, in these later offences he had also used threats and a degree of force to secure compliance. Those responsible for supervising him in the community had thought he was 'doing well'.

It transpired, however, that despite presenting favourably to his supervisors he had been involved for many months in serious sexual misconduct. He was recalled from the community and sent to hospital. He subsequently appeared in court charged with the new series of offences. Once again he was given a further psychiatric disposal and he remains in hospital. Like many other people of his disposition, Peter is a 'model' patient. Sadly, this affords no measure of optimism for those entrusted with his management to conclude that he has changed his basic sexual orientation. His psychopathic condition is in fact regarded as untreatable.

Should Peter have been awarded a further psychiatric disposal at his last court appearance? Would a prison sentence have been more appropriate? In other words is he mad or bad or both? And how does one estimate his future dangerousness?

Vignette 4: The Arsonist

'Margaret' had a preoccupation with fire. She was in her mid-forties and serving a life sentence for her third conviction for arson with intent to endanger life. Like a number of arsonists I have met, she had shown such a preoccupation from childhood.

Margaret also had a history of making hoax calls to the fire service and gradually became increasingly involved in fire-setting behaviour. At various times she had been given several different diagnoses, for example severe personality disorder, depressive disorder and schizophrenia. No psychiatric professional had considered that she easily fulfilled any of the criteria for a single, clear-cut diagnosis. She had spent periods of time in both ordinary psychiatric and secure psychiatric hospitals and units. In these establishments she had been both aggressive and disruptive; and in states of tension would seek to resolve these by setting fires.

The circumstances of the offence for which Margaret had received her life sentence were that she considered that her fellow residents in the after-care hostel where they were all residing were 'ganging-up' on her. One evening, when they and the duty member of staff had gone to bed she poured a large quantity of paraffin over the furniture and set light to it. She used a fuse made from rags soaked in the same liquid. She then left the premises. Fortunately, the smoke detector in the lounge alerted the other residents. However, a number of them suffered from the effects of smoke inhalation and needed hospital treatment. Over the years, many and varied approaches were tried with Margaret but these had met with only a very modest degree of success. Because of this, psychiatrists who gave evidence at her trial were unanimous in their view that her condition was not treatable within the terms of the mental health legislation.

In sentencing her to life imprisonment, the judge commented on her actual and potential dangerousness. He indicated that she would not be released until those responsible for her management considered she was safe for such a course to be implemented. Those working in the socio-forensic field know only too well just how difficult such predictions are to make.

Vignette 5: A Borderline Case

'Gideon' was a 26-year-old African-Caribbean man. He was considered by some psychiatric professionals to suffer from a form of schizophrenia that made him highly suspicious of other people and liable to engage in violence whenever he felt affronted or frustrated.

It is important to record that Gideon lived in an area where his fellow African-Caribbean citizens complained that they felt very alienated and also that they were 'picked upon' more frequently by the police than were their white peers of a similar age. It seems likely that his illness had been deemed to play a more significant role as a determinant of his behaviour than was justified by the facts. Gideon's behaviour and its origins raise important issues concerning the interface between psychiatry and the law.

Vignette 6: Serendipity

'William' was in his late forties and had been charged with attempting to murder his wife by cutting her throat while she lay asleep. He was normally an extremely docile and placid person. William was a mechanic by trade and said to be an excellent workman. It transpired that his wife had for some years worked as a prostitute. Despite all her husband's entreaties, she refused to abandon this lifestyle. In a fit of anger and despair he attacked her, but in view of what the judge regarded as unusual and extenuating circumstances he passed a comparatively light sentence of imprisonment, of five years. The case could of course have ended more tragically; his wife could well have died from her injuries.

In other cases, only the fact that the assailant had been interrupted during the assault might have limited the harm caused. In yet others, the intention might not have been to kill or cause serious injury, but factors unknown to the perpetrator might render the outcome tragic. For example, the victim might be infirm or have a very thin skull, or the emergency or medical services might have difficulties reaching the crime scene. So how to assess madness, badness or dangerousness if chance plays a part?

Comment

The vignettes highlight a number of problems in drawing firm lines of demarcation between normality, madness and badness. In addition they illustrate some of the problems involved in finding suitable and effective modes of management. They also demonstrate the need to distinguish between those who have a high nuisance value and those whose behaviour may have a more malignant side. In order to approach all these matters, professionals may also find that they have to confront their own 'demons'!

Acknowledgements

In the somewhat fragmentary recollections in this book I have called upon (perhaps 'dredged up' would be a better description) the memories of a variety of friends and colleagues. If my recollections and interpretations are faulty in any respect I proffer my apologies; any corrections or amplifications will be gratefully received. As this book is more a personal than an academic account, I have kept referencing to a minimum. My continuing thanks to Mrs. Janet Kirkwood for producing such excellent 'copy' from my quite unprofessional drafts and to Bryan Gibson and his staff for their support in this venture.

Herschel Prins

December 2009
Universities of Leicester and Loughborough

Dedication

For Norma, my wife of over fifty years,
and other members of my family,
past and present.

About the author

Herschel Prins has worked in the criminal justice and forensic mental health fields for over five decades, including as a probation officer, psychiatric social worker and Home Office Inspector of Probation. He also served on various statutory sector and voluntary sector bodies, including the Parole Board, Mental Health Review Tribunal and Mental Health Act Commission. He teaches at Leicester University and Loughborough University and holds a professorial appointment at each.

For several years, Herschel Prins chaired the Nacro Committee on Mentally Disordered Offenders. He also served on committees of the Howard League and the Institute For the Study and Treatment of Delinquency.[1] He was a member of the editorial boards of several academic and professional journals as well as writing some dozen books and around 200 papers for academic and professional journals (a number of which are noted in the text).

Herschel Prins chaired three inquiries in the mental health arena. These included that into the death of Orville Blackwood at Broadmoor Hospital and a homicide committed by a patient 'known to the psychiatric and allied services' in Leicester. In recognition of a lifetime of achievements in this sphere of public affairs, the Herschel Prins Low Secure Centre at the Glenfield Hospital, Leicester bears his name.

The author of the Foreword

David Wilson is Professor of Criminology at the Centre of Applied Criminology, Birmingham City University. A former prison governor, he is the editor of the *Howard Journal* and a regular broadcaster and presenter, including for the BBC, Channel 4 and Sky Television. A leading expert on crime and punishment, he has written several books in this sphere, including (for Waterside Press) *Prison(er) Education* (with Ann Reuss), *Images of Incarceration* (with Sean O'Sullivan) (2004) and *Serial Killers* (2007).

---

1. The ISTD has since become the Centre for Crime and Justice Studies (CCJS).

CHAPTER ONE

Introduction and Early Memories[1]

The opportunity to look back over a career in crime and forensic mental health of well over fifty years is likely to be a comparatively rare event and, let it be said, may prove to be a mixed blessing. One may be accused of a degree of vanity and self-advertisement and of having mixed motives. However, one's less happy experiences may also need to be aired before catharsis is achieved and 'ghosts' laid to rest. In my teaching of numerous professionals, and those who aspire to that role, I have often spoken of the need to confront one's own 'demons' – and I cannot exclude myself from that need. This therapeutic aspiration is well summed up by Banquo in *Macbeth*. When Duncan's murder is discovered, and before the *dramatis personae* go their separate ways, he makes the following trenchant statement:

> And when we have our naked frailties hid that suffer in exposure, let us meet to question this most bloody business further' (*Macbeth*, Act 2, Sc.iii, lines 119-122).

Some brief comments on how my decision to write this account came about seem to be justified. Way back in July, 2005 I had to respond briefly as the recipient of an Honorary Doctorate in Science from Loughborough University; I have worked part time

---

1. Shortened versions of some of the material in this chapter have appeared in: Prins, H. (2007), 'Fifty Years' Hard Labour (A Personal Odyssey)', *The Howard Journal of Criminal Justice*, 46(2): pp 176-193; (2008) 'Historical Commentary: Half a Century of Madness and Badness: Some Diverse Recollections', *The Journal of Forensic Psychiatry and Psychology*, 19(4): pp 431-440; and (2010) *Chapter 1* in: *Offenders, Deviants or Patients?: Explorations in Clinical Criminology*, (4th ed.), London: Routledge (in press). See also: Jones. C. (2007) 'Biography: Herschel Prins', *The Journal of Forensic Psychiatry and Psychology*, 18(1): pp 127-133.

in the Midlands Centre for Criminology and Criminal Justice (Department of Social Sciences) for nearly twenty years. In his letter of guidance, our then Vice-Chancellor – Professor Sir David Wallace – advised me that my response should last no longer than three to four minutes – adding that the young graduates and their families could become somewhat restless if one went on for too long! I found that my draft (which I had the good sense to send to David Wallace) came out at nearly ten. He 'phoned me with his customary good humour and asked me to cut it by fifty percent! In doing so (and subsequently) he had suggested that my account would profit from extension and elaboration for a wider audience. In this he was supported by various friends and colleagues.

This eventually led to the further suggestion that some short notes I had made concerning my varied experiences could be developed, extended and turned into a more permanent record in the form of a book. Hence the present 'offering'. In trying to shape it I have opted for a fairly sequential account – preferring this to following a somewhat arbitrary selection of topics.

EARLY YEARS

Like many fellow professionals I believe that early (and notably family) experiences can shape our later destinies. For this reason I have always stressed to the wide range of students I have taught over the years that you cannot really understand and manage present behaviour unless you endeavour to locate it in past experiences. As a young child I recall my father maintaining that our Dutch ancestors held positions of some influence in our country of origin – Holland. As I grew up I came to view my father's recollections with a degree of mild scepticism. However, a communication two or three years ago from a hitherto unknown second (or maybe third) cousin, with an impressive interest in genealogy, indicated that my father's statements may have had a modicum of truth to them, since cousin Martyn (resident in Australia) had delved deeply into our ancestry and found evidence of positions of some influence back to the early sixteen hundreds.

I was an only child and, like many only children, I experienced the emotional impact of such sole status. There are indications that my not so young parents had tried for children for some time, and that at least one previous pregnancy had resulted in a still-birth. I can recall that my parents (particularly my mother) were, with hindsight, solicitous to the point of over-protectiveness. The extent to which this over-protectiveness was in part generated by her less than happy experience of pregnancy, or her life-long indifferent ill-health, remains a matter for conjecture. However, I have no doubt that such an environment has contributed to a degree of mild hypochondriasis on my part. Other influences contributed to my interest in mental ill-health and criminality, and I shall consider these shortly.

On reaching what today would be regarded as primary school age I attended a nearby 'kindergarten' school in Finchley (London). This was presided over by two joint headmistresses – Miss Shanklin and Miss Dunham. As I recall, Miss Shanklin was a fairly shadowy (but very benign) woman. Miss Dunham on the other hand seemed more powerful and from my point of view an intimidating figure. In truth, she scared me and, as a consequence, I learned very little from her and I ascribe my life-long aversion to matters mathematical to her unhelpful and derogatory attitude.

The time came for me to take the Eleven Plus exam, which I promptly failed (but by what margin I know not). Success in the Eleven Plus would have afforded me entry to the local (and well regarded) Christ's College. Failure meant that I *could* have gone to the somewhat less prestigious, and more distant, comparable school (Finchley County). Being wartime, my protective parents did not opt for this choice, but arranged for me to attend a local fee-paying school – Ravensfield College. Under non-wartime circumstances this, like my 'primary school, would have been under the joint headship of Mr. Sowter and Mr. Cooke. However, the latter was away on war service. Peter Sowter (or 'Pius' as we less than reverent schoolchildren chose to call him – his initials standing for Peter Ian Unwin). My earliest recollection of Pius was being interviewed by him prior to my acceptance. Whilst the exact recollections of this interview have been repressed, one clear memory stands out, that of his highly skilled and sensitive piano playing and of his asking me if I liked 'classical' music. I cannot recall what answer I gave (too tongue-tied I guess). However, I now believe that his interest in music, and the piano recitals he gave for us, sowed the seeds of my later keen interest in music (though I have never learned to *play* an instrument). Pius arranged piano recitals for the school, and one or two were given by the late Edith Vogel – a pianist of some distinction

Being war-time, some of the younger teachers had gone off on war service. Those that remained were quite an interesting bunch, some more advanced in their pedagogic views than others. I warmed very considerably to one or two of them. We were taught Latin by a Dutchmen – Mr. Van Kronenberg – and I was sorry (as was he) that I was not able to study it far enough to take it as a subject in the (then) School Certificate exam. He had a fine sense of humour and always responded with good humour to our teasing about his girlfriend in the Women's Royal Air Force (who I think he married subsequently). For her sins (if she had any, which I doubt) Miss Ida Busbridge taught us both maths and history. I let her down badly by failing my maths miserably, but brought pleasure to her in her other subject – history – which I passed with distinction. (I have often wondered if she was the same Ida Busbridge who became a Reader in Mathematics at Cambridge. I would like to think so).

Pius taught us geography. The degree to which this was a pleasant or an awesome experience depended on his mood. On a bad day he could be irritable and even aggressive with the occasional flight of the blackboard eraser across the room! In my later days at Ravensfield we were taught by the gifted Mrs. Adosides – English herself, but married to a Greek husband. My subsequent interest in the Bard, and of literature more generally, owes much to her imaginative teaching and example. We acted Shakespeare in the classroom instead of being passive chair-bound readers. Finally, I should mention Mr. Lancelot Baker. He taught both Latin and French. Corrections to our written efforts were rewarded (or rather punished) by two symbols. A blue square for a minor error and a red square for a more heinous grammatical one. This was punished by a 'slippering'. Another of his somewhat questionable practices was his routine and regular weighing and measuring of our youthful persons. We were required to be in a state of more or less complete undress for these 'examinations'. I recall that my father went out of his way to question the need for this somewhat unusual extra-curricular activity. I surmise that today his activities would certainly have been regarded as paedo-philic in nature. As far as I am aware, no inquiries were ever made about these. On the credit side, he did a lot to encourage drama in the school and put on some well received plays. My talents in this direction were rewarded by acting (jointly) as assistant stage manager! Had it not been for the last minute defection of the leading man in our production of *Macbeth*, I would have trodden the boards as first witch and first murderer – perhaps the first indication of my later interest in forensic matters. Having been afflicted from childhood with quite an intrusive stammer, I found that like many stammerers it ceased to become a problem when acting or singing (which I did very badly and was banned as a 'growler' in the so-called school choir)!

Towards the end of my days at Ravensfield I participated in what, at the time, was an innovative practice. Senior pupils at the end of the summer term were allowed to run the school for a day and devise such activities as they wished, provided they did not outrage decency! I chose to subject the school and staff to a giant quiz. For obvious reasons of equity the quiz had to be of a very general nature, and it was good that the staff had to pit their wits against the pupils.

TWO FAMILY DEATHS

My immediate post-school destiny was to be clouded considerably by the deaths in quick succession of both my parents.

My father had fought in the First World War, achieving commissioned rank and having some involvement in the development and use of the early tanks. He received severe shrapnel wounds and his left arm was so badly damaged that a return to his pre-war occupation in the diamond setting business as a mounter was not possible. Some of his brothers had also been involved in this business; one was killed in the conflict and another had experienced severe frost-bite to his feet. As a small child I was fascinated by my father's war wounds – I called them his 'tramlines'. Through a family connection with the late Sir Basil Henriques my father was appointed as the 'Superintendent' of the Jewish Discharged Prisoners' Aid Society.

No particular qualifications seem to have been required for this post. No doubt, in those far off days, his army service and 'a command of men' were seen as sufficient attributes. According to his accounts of his work he seems to have dealt with a range of pretty devious (and sometimes dangerous) characters, thus giving the lie to the frequently held belief that Jews were always highly law-abiding members of the community! He had a collection of various weapons that he had allegedly taken from some of his 'customers'. His employing committee considered that he needed two assistants to carry out his rehabilitative work. One was the sturdy Mr. Anning (who was, as I recall, a retired police officer), and Mr. Binstock who acted as an office manager and general factotum.

Events in the Second World War took their toll on my father's health. His brother, sister-in-law, their two children and two cousins were all killed in an air raid. My father was called upon to identify the bodies, which were almost unrecognizable.

Although I believe there was a powerful 'genetic' element in the development of his heart disease (his father had died from heart trouble at an early age) the war pressures had undoubtedly taken their toll. His health deteriorated, culminating in a serious heart attack which killed him. Having suffered two serious heart attacks myself in the early nineteen eighties, this possible genetic element of heart disease on the paternal side of my family has been borne in upon me over the years. The fact that I have 'lived (so far) to tell the tale' says much for chemotherapeutic developments since my father's illness. Much criticism is often laid at the door of the pharmaceutical industry. I counter this by pointing out to such critics that had the various anti-hypertensive and other drugs been available in my father's day he *might* have lived much longer than he did (he died in his late fifties).

I recall that my mother had always been in somewhat indifferent health. Her mother (Grandma Abbie) always claimed that she was a distant relative of Alfred Mendoza, the famous bareknuckle boxer. It is my surmise that my mother never really recovered from my father's sudden death in the face of an anticipated full recovery from his heart disease. It was as though she had given up the desire to go on living. During her last and fatal illness I stayed with one of her sisters and family. Visiting her in hospital almost daily, I watched her gradually fade away. I recall that the official cause of her death was malignant kidney failure. A nonmedical view might be that she died of a 'broken heart'. I have never explored in any depth my deepest feelings about her death (or, for that matter, my father's) but I'm sure that my feelings of largely unexpressed sorrow must have been mixed with resentment at being left an orphan in my mid-teens.

Following their deaths, two important choices had to be made. First, decisions about any further education and subsequent employment and, second, where would I live? Despite a most generous offer from an elderly childless neighbour and his wife that they would be very happy to subsidise my continuing education, the question was decided in highly autocratic fashion by my mother's late brother Harry. This was that I should enter the world of work. He used his influence to secure employment for me at the Scholl Manufacturing Company as a trainee surgical instrument maker. (Scholls are perhaps better known for their orthopaedic footwear). Subsequent events confounded my uncle's assumption that I had the necessary skills. My performance at their factory fell far short of requirement.

Even at this great distance of time, it shames me to think how many pairs of Spencer-Wells (artery forceps) I must have ruined at the work-bench, this despite the kindly, if occasionally impatient, guidance from the foreman – Mr. Arnold. I think several of my younger work companions were sympathetic about my lack of manual dexterity and I formed a brief friendship with Albert (a bit older than me) and his older brother. They took me along to union meetings and I did become (for a time) a paid up member of the Amalgamated Engineering Union!

My ineptitude having been recognized, I was eventually 'transferred' to the company's offices. Here, under the guidance of the highly efficient Miss Bridle and her junior colleagues Miss Chapman and Mr. Ferrari, I was introduced to the intricacies of the purchase of raw materials, seeing to their delivery and that payment for them had been made. My other duties included making small personal purchases at the behest of one of the two UK Directors of the Company – a Mr. Temy – a kindly man, who had responded to my uncle's initial request to find employment for me.

On one notable occasion I let him down fairly badly. It was at this time that the now ubiquitous 'ballpoint' (Biros) came on the scene. Refills for these pens, made by the Miles Martin Company, were somewhat difficult to obtain. It was in the course of one of these transactions that I made a serious error of judgement. I was entrusted with a package that needed to be sent by registered post. I did not realise that such a package had to be sent via the post office and receipted. I merely popped it in the post box.

Imagine my discomfort when, upon my return to the office, I was asked for the receipt! Happily the item in question reached its destination safely. Having received a reputation in later life for a high degree of efficiency, I thought it only right to indicate that this was not always the case. Idols do often have feet of clay as I tell my students!

WHERE TO LIVE?

Both sides of my parents' families needed to decide where I ought to live. Fortunately, I was afforded some choice in the matter (unlike the decision-making process in respect of my further education and employment). Had not both sides of the family shown a degree of willingness to take me in, I could well have ended up in an orphanage and become a charge on the State. (The question concerning my future 'location' arose before the passing and implementation of the Children Act 1948).[2] I chose

2. The pioneering Children Act of 1948 arose out of a growing concern about the plight of orphaned and disadvantaged children; the specific 'spur' for change was the case of young Dennis O'Neil, killed by his foster-father. The case was highlighted in a powerful letter to *The Times* by Lady Allen of Hurtwood. In the

the option of going to live with my late father's family, feeling that I would be more comfortable with them. I reached this (subsequently very wise) decision on the basis of having lived with some of my mother's family following my father's death. This experience was not entirely to our liking and I have always assumed that she would have approved of my decision.

My father's immediate family in Hendon consisted of his younger unmarried brother (Bernard), his sisters Henrietta (Yetta) a widow (who was *de facto* the mother following the demise at a relatively early age of my paternal grandfather), aunts Phoebe, Rebecca and Sarah and Yetta's daughter Hannah. All unmarried except for Yetta. (Rebecca subsequently married very late in life).

On reflection I'm not at all sure that they appreciated the implications of taking an adolescent into their home. However, they showed great understanding in accepting my occasional bursts of intolerance and waywardness. For my part, I showed my gratitude by becoming quite adept at domestic chores and DIY skills, both of which have subsequently stood me in good stead over the years. My prolonged stay with them also probably contributed much to my understanding of, and empathy towards, the older generation.

When eventually I married my wife Norma and we had our two children Helen and Jeremy, my aunts and uncles became a group of loving secondary grandparents alongside Norma's

light of the boy's death, and by Lady Allen's letter, a Committee was established under the chairmanship of Dame Myra Curtis. The Committee advocated a new and specifically designated Children's (Local Authority) Department under the directorship of a Children's Officer. This separate service remained in force until the reorganization of Social Services following the reports of the Younghusband and Seebohm Committees, when social care services were combined into single departments. As a result of this, the care of children had to compete for resources with the care of the mentally ill and handicapped, the physically disabled and the elderly. A much more recent change has resulted in children's services being incorporated into education provision. *Plus ça change!*

mother and father. This conjunction brought much happin╌
all sides. There is little doubt that my early and later familial ex╌
riences had a marked influence on my subsequent career choice
as I will explain later.

THE ROYAL AIR FORCE

The immediate post-war years witnessed a continuation of
National Service. As a consequence, I found myself conscripted
into the Royal Air Force in late 1946. Normally one's national
service would have been for one or two years, but a number of
us were subjected to an extended three months because of the
Berlin Airlift.[3] Initially, I had aspirations of becoming a radar
operator, but my lack of mathematical ability as demonstrated on
the RAF's tests showed quite forcibly that this was not to be. I was
thus designated to be a clerk/telephonist.

Believing that one should make as much legitimate use of
one's 'infirmities' as possible, I managed to convince the officer
in charge of the allocation of new entrants - a Wing Commander
Smith - that my fairly mild stammer would make me somewhat
less than competent as a telephone operator! I was therefore
regarded as a clerk/general duties which satisfied me greatly.

My enthusiasm for this new designation must have spurred
me on to great efforts because I came out 'top' (as a leading
aircraftsman (LAC)) at the conclusion of my four weeks training
course. Following a variety of postings I ended my service at RAF
Digby in Lincolnshire – a unit adjacent to the Royal Air Force
College at Cranwell. Somewhat to my surprise, I was eventually
promoted to the rank of acting corporal (paid). As 'acting' posts
were not normally paid, this was a decided bonus.

[3.] The maintenance of an air corridor for flights into West Berlin after the Soviet
bloc for a time stopped all other means of access to that part of the city.

Service in the RAF was certainly a very 'broadening' experience. One met with some very bigoted and mildly sadistic NCOs, rampant anti-semitism, sexism, and homosexual advances. Despite all these negatives, some firm and lasting friendships were forged and I also met some very sympathetic senior officers of whom Group Captain Seymour, our Commanding Officer at Digby, was an excellent example. However, two plus years was enough and I was not displeased to return to 'civvy street'.

AN INTERIM PERIOD

It became necessary to find some kind of 'interim' employment during which time I could consider what I wanted to do with my life. Happily (the exact circumstances now escape me) I found a congenial clerical post at a locally based Ministry of Transport Depot. My immediate boss was a Mr. Kessel – a kindly European immigrant, and the depot manager was equally kind. I recall the latter was a keen speedway enthusiast, and was very supportive during my second (and thankfully successful) attempt to pass the (then) Group G motor-cycle test. I had more luck at a later date with the motor car driving test – passing first time. I'm not so sure I would be as successful today if I had to take what has become a much more challenging test.

During this period of my life I began to contemplate what direction my future career should take. In the final months of my stay in the RAF I was able to go on a month's 'pre-teacher training course' held at RAF Kenley in Surrey. At this time my stammer was not too problematic; I enjoyed the course and received a very encouraging report at its conclusion. The RAF NCO in charge – Sgt. Roland Jones – encouraged me to consider training as a teacher. I did in fact apply to one or two colleges, but was not successful in any of my applications. With hindsight, this was probably something of a blessing and meant that generations of school children were mercifully saved from my attempts to educate them. The chapters that follow attempt to trace some of the later experiences that I regard as significant during the development of my professional career. I consider this first chapter as being important, since some of the events described have been influential in contributing to my career choices. Further formative influences will be apparent in what follows.

CHAPTER TWO

First Professional Steps

That there was some history of engagement in social welfare activity in my family is evidenced by my father's occupation with the Jewish Discharged Prisoners' Aid Society (*Chapter 1*). In addition, my father's brother (Bernard) and his sister (Sarah) had been close working colleagues of the late Sir Basil Henriques - the well-known London juvenile court magistrate. Bernard had played an important role in the activities of the Oxford and Saint George's Settlement Youth Clubs situated in the Bernhard Baron Settlement in London's East End.

OTHER POINTERS TO A CAREER

Sarah had originally trained as a teacher and worked subsequently as Sir Basil's secretary. During the time I lived with Bernard and Sarah their activities took a somewhat different course. Sarah became the organizing secretary of the League of Jewish Women and Bernard the boys' after-care secretary at what was then known as the Norwood Jewish Orphanage.

My subsequent interest in mental health matters probably owes some of its origins to the circumstances of two of my other aunts. Aunt Yetta had married a close relative (her uncle) who was several years her senior. The wedding had taken place in Holland as, at that time, it would not have been recognized as a lawful union in the UK. My first cousin was the product of their union. It is not altogether surprising that as she developed, she exhibited a number of psycho-physical problems which took the form of severe hypochondria and phantasising.

Later in her life, and whilst living in America, she married an America citizen and she lived out her days in that country. For many years she was wheel-chair bound and needed crutches when not in the chair. To the best of my knowledge no clearly established physical causes were found to account for her condition. It was, to my mind, brought about by a combination of genetic and environmental causes.

Another of my aunts - Rebecca - had suffered for many years from what today would probably be described as a bipolar disorder, and she was only helped by supportive psycho-analytic psychotherapy. I have no doubt that the lives of both these relatives helped to shape my later interest in mental health matters.

By way of contrast, my mother's family showed no interest in professional social welfare (though my mother herself was always very supportive of my father's work and engaged in some 'good works' herself). At the point at which I was seeking admission to social science diploma courses, her side of the family (mainly through Harry) tried actively to dissuade me. I recall that Bernard and Sarah had a somewhat bruising encounter with the latter.

Subsequent events proved that Harry was something of an undesirable person. Taking control of a flourishing retail and wholesale tobacconist's business from my late grandfather, he ended up virtually squandering it, and my late cousin (Lionel) had to work hard to re-establish it after Harry died. It also seems that he looked for pleasure in places other than the marital bed. His relationships with his wife and three children (my cousins) never seemed to me to be particularly happy. Sadly one of his daughters committed suicide following her mother's death.

SOCIAL WORK EDUCATION

Undeterred and with Sarah and Bernard's quiet encouragement, I began to seek information about social science courses. My path led me to the kindly (but slightly austere) respected figure of Mr. Benjamin Astbury, who was the General Secretary of the well-regarded Family Welfare Association. His knowledge of, and advice concerning, various courses was invaluable. I eventually secured a place at what was then the South West Essex Technical College. Sheffield University had been suggested as another possibility, but I did not pursue this since I had been away from home for a considerable time when in the RAF. The principal of the college was doctor Harry Lowry - an accomplished organist. He gave lunchtime recitals and I suspect that these helped to develop my growing interest in music. Both Sarah and Bernard were 'into' classical music and had quite a good collection of old '78's which I played on an old 'wind-up' gramophone. Such enthusiasm! The membership of our two-year course was small, and fortunately we all got on very well together. Our course tutor - Miss Strachan Cousins - kept a quiet but benign eye upon us and taught social administration.

Public administration was taught by Miss Green; her course included the administration of justice - both civil and criminal - a useful background as it happens for my later career choice. Mr. Jones taught us economics; I recall with some amusement, his efforts to teach us the rudiments of the law of marginal utility through a consideration of slices of toast! However, for my part the most influential teacher on the course was the late Dr. Paul Halmos (later a professor at Cardiff University and then the Open University).

Paul Halmos taught us social psychology. He managed to cover the prescribed syllabus in less than the allotted time and was able to add in several additional topics that he thought would interest us. Sadly, a fatal heart attack cut short his career at the Open University. Paul was an original thinker, a powerful intellect, and a sensitive teacher. He encouraged me to consider working with what were then called 'maladjusted children'. He had links with the well regarded Mulberry Bush School, run by the redoubtable Mrs. Docker-Drysdale. Although aspects of this work appealed to me, I felt I needed something with a broader base and applied to the Home Office for probation training. Part of my motivation for this field of work arose out of a 'placement' I had undertaken as part of my social science course. I was attached to a slightly eccentric but well experienced tutor – John McFarlane. He was a most stimulating individual as were his colleagues, including the senior probation officer, Mr. Sharp. Other field placements on the course included a residential placement with the children's Country Holiday Fund; an informal but very insight-promoting experience. My third placement was not quite so happy. It was with a local office of the Family Welfare Association (FWA). I was supervised by a somewhat formidable lady – Miss Gruber – who sadly I never really got to like or understand. Occasionally I took 'refuge' by talking to the delightful and insightful Lily Pincus, the author of a seminal book entitled *Death and the Family*. Mrs. Pincus was employed by a Marital Therapy Organization Family Discussion Bureau with offices in the same building as the FWA.

To return to probation training. Even in the early nineteen-fifties the selection process was quite sophisticated, based largely on tests designed by the National Institute For Industrial Psychology. The first part of my selection process was with a very friendly and relaxed Home Office Probation Inspector, the late Selby Barrett (who was to later become a colleague and close family friend). Having survived his scrutiny, I went forward for the intelligence tests and participation in a group discussion which was observed by the final interview panel of three members. I recall these three 'wise persons' as being very informal, but quite shrewd! I'm sure not much passed them unobserved.

PROBATION TRAINING

I managed to pass muster and was selected for probation training shortly afterwards in late 1951. The Home Office specialist course was organized and run by members of the Probation Inspectorate (much later to be designated as *Her Majesty's Inspectorate*, a designation and status emphasising its independence, but still then located within the Home Office[1] and, no doubt, to bring it into line with, for example, Her Majesty's Inspectorate of Education and similar governmental inspectorates such as those relating to factories).

The course was divided into three parts. An initial field-work placement, a period of residence at Rainer House off London's Sloane Square, and a second field-work placement. The house was run under the auspices of the Rainer Foundation,[2] taking its name from one John Rainer – an early probation pioneer in the United States.[3] Little did I realise at the time that some ten years later I would find *myself* in the inspectorate and involved in running similar courses. Thinking back, the Home Office course provided

1. It is now associated with the later Ministry of Justice.
2. Now known as 'Catch 22' into which it was incorporated in 2009.
3. It seems appropriate to note here a very short history of the development of the Probation Service. As early as 1820, the Warwickshire Quarter Sessions adopted the practice of passing a sentence of one day's imprisonment on a youthful offender on condition that he returned to his parent or 'master' (employer). Some years later the Recorder of Portsmouth added a degree of enforcement to the practice by requiring sureties for good behaviour. In the second half of the nineteenth century voluntary agencies began to play an active role in these developments, leading to the work of the Police Court Mission under the aegis of the Church of England Temperance Society. Their original work was in the London Magistrates' Courts. All these developments led to the eventual statutory implementation of probation as a penal measure under the Probation of Offenders Act of 1907. This enactment was further enlarged by the Criminal Justice Act of 1948. The original welfare-orientated ethos of the 1907 and 1948 Acts of 'advising, assisting and befriending' has now, sadly, virtually disappeared under modern-day legislation. (For more detailed accounts of the inception and development of the service, see Prins, 1960, 1964 and 2007).

a very sound foundation for probation work. Our inspector/
tutors were not only kindly and supportive, but clearly able
people. I regard my contact with them on the course, and later
as colleagues, as having had a deep and lasting influence on my
professional development. Our teachers from 'outside' the Home
Office were a group of distinguished academics and clinicians. I
recall, amongst others, Dr Hermann Mannheim from the London
School of Economics, who taught criminology and penology, and
Dr (later Professor) Trevor Gibbens, who taught psychiatric aspects
of delinquency. We also attended pretty demanding 'case-work'
seminars at the home of the distinguished psychoanalytic psychiatrist, Dr Dennis Carroll. The delightful and visually impaired A.
C. L. Morrison (of *Clark Hall and Morrison on Children* fame)
lectured to us on law at Bow Street Magistrates' Court.

As a group we were youthful, but the course did include a leav-
ening of more mature entrants. I recall that the 'mix' had benefits for both parties. I think we behaved reasonably well, though
perhaps not always to the entire satisfaction of the lady warden.
Scottish country dancing (promoted by one of the female course
members) was highly popular, though on one occasion our activities threatened damage to the dining room ceiling. Occasional
'forays' were also popular. I recall a somewhat 'scary' drive
to Brighton in a series of heavy snow storms. Not all personal
encounters ended up so happily. I remember that one older course
member from overseas was asked to leave the course following a
complaint from a female member of the course concerning an
unwelcome sexual advance in a theatre. On a more pleasant note,
a number of lasting friendships were made, one or two of them
ending in marriage. One of my early 'serious' girl friends was a
fellow course member; a relationship that ended by her decision
to return to her previous long-term boyfriend!

In what was in those days a very small service - one of its
attractions - a number of course members went on to achieve

prominence as senior or chief officers in the service. Inevitably, not all course members stayed in the service; one of the female members I got to know very well chose marriage to a farmer and life on a fairly remote Scottish island.

PLACEMENTS

As indicated earlier, the practical element of the course consisted of two fieldwork placements. The first was the shorter of the two. Mine was in Shropshire under the careful and supportive tutelage of a very congenial supervisor – Ivor Llewellyn. (Ivor subsequently left the service to go into child care work; I like to think I wasn't the 'final straw' in that decision!) Shropshire was my first serious experience of rural England and I thoroughly enjoyed my time there.

The second, and somewhat more extended, placement was at the City of Portsmouth Probation Office under the supervision of Jack Lovatt, the principal probation officer. I discovered subsequently that it was somewhat unusual for principal officers to act as tutor officers (later to be termed supervisors). I have always suspected that I was sent to him because the Home Office had discerned a degree of youthful exuberance which needed some level of 'kindly containment'. In today's climate of detailed fieldwork assessment procedures it is interesting to recall that in those early days the Home Office used a 'check-list' of tasks to be covered which the trainee took from one placement to the next. The list was very comprehensive, and served as a helpful reminder of the functions that needed to be covered and assessed. Jack Lovatt provided me with a great deal of wise guidance and I have always counted myself fortunate in having had the opportunity, not only to be supervised by him, but to gain some insights into the role and function of a chief officer. (I don't think Jack would have felt much at home today with the present role of a chief officer).

I found Portsmouth to be an interesting city. It is, of course, a port and naval centre. As well as heterosexual prostitution, it saw a good deal of illicit sexual activity between men which, at that time, led to court appearances and sentences for both the importuners and the importuned. Happily, the criminalisation of such encounters between adults in private was to disappear from the Statute Book (see also *Chapter 11*).

In the following chapter I recall my experiences on moving to Bedfordshire where I undertook my first work as a fully qualified probation officer

CHAPTER THREE

A Rural Sojourn

Although there was no actual 'direction' by the Home Office regarding employment, there was some degree of light-handed 'guidance' by our Tutors at Rainer House. My first post, in 1952, was as a probation officer in Bedfordshire. The formal interviews for such posts in those days could be a somewhat intimidating experience.

INTERVIEW AND APPOINTMENT

I recall being seated in the Council Chamber at County Hall and facing representatives from all the petty sessional divisions (the then name for court areas) in the county. In total, there must have been at least twenty five of these representatives - all of them entitled to ask the candidates questions! To make matters worse, I was almost blinded by the sun streaming through the stained glass windows, so that I needed to squint at my interrogators.

Today, such interviews, though rigorous, are conducted by a small sub-committee of the probation authority (the Probation Board). I survived the ordeal and was offered a post stationed in Bedford. I had applied originally for a post being advertised in the south of the county – at Dunstable. It would appear that the 'powers that be' considered that the degree of 'youthful exuberance' identified in training needed a continuing degree of oversight from more experienced colleagues.

As it transpired, my fellow applicant, who was appointed to the Dunstable post, seemed equally in need of friendly oversight, as he came to be regarded as having somewhat eccentric ideas. Our need for friendly guidance brought us fairly close together and my colleague and his wife became firm friends. Eventually, he decided that he needed a change of direction, and he joined the rapidly developing child care service.

THE CRIMINAL JUSTICE ACT 1948: A NOTE

Work as a probation officer in those distant days needs to be seen against the background of changes brought into being by the Criminal Justice Act of 1948.

The Act had appeared as a Bill in 1939, but was shelved as a result of the advent of the Second World War. The 1948 Act has always seemed to me to be something of a milestone in the history of criminal justice administration in England and Wales. In my view, its importance appears to have been somewhat neglected in the accounts of its inception and subsequent development. (I recently 'quizzed' some of my post-graduate criminology students as to their knowledge of this Act. They seem to have barely heard of it!).

The Act abolished flogging as a penalty (except for assaults on prison staff - where the penalty was also subsequently abolished). It ushered in the new sentences of corrective training (CT) and preventive detention (PD) for so-called 'habitual criminals' (a provision first introduced in the Prevention of Crime Act 1908), and detention centres and attendance centres (both of these for youths and young adults). It is of interest to note that subsequent statutory provisions have continued the practice of preventive incarceration. For example, the introduction of the 'extended sentence' in the nineteen-sixties and, much more recently, the powers to impose such sentences in cases of serious offending (such as those involving violence) through the Criminal Justice Act 2003 and subsequent amendments to it.

From my point of view, one of the most important provisions of the 1948 Act was that it made it possible for those offenders showing milder forms of mental disorder to receive treatment for their condition as in-patients or out-patients for a period not exceeding three years.

The offender had to consent to the order and there had to be medical evidence supporting such a penalty. Subsequent enactments (for example, the Criminal Justice Act of 1967) introduced parole on a statutory basis, community service and the deferred sentence. I should also note here that at the time of the 1939 Bill, plans had been made for the introduction of a psychiatric prison – eventually Grendon Underwood (now just plain Grendon) Prison. Overall this has been a successful enterprise - to the extent that a 'second Grendon' has been established.

BACK TO REALITY IN BEDFORDSHIRE

To return to Bedfordshire. I recall arriving on an Easter Bank Holiday in April, 1952. Lodgings had been found for me by my close colleague to be - the late Geoffrey Brunson - father of Michael Brunson, the one-time BBC newscaster and commentator. The probation office in Bedford High Street had been opened up for me - despite it being a Bank Holiday! Much to my dismay, I discovered that two home surroundings reports (as they were then labelled) on juveniles were required to be undertaken for presentation at the Biggleswade Juvenile Court that Wednesday.

A degree of panic overtook me! The Tuesday was spent undertaking the inquiries in the large village of Sandy (home of the Royal Society for the Protection of Birds) and getting them typed up by the senior office secretary on the Wednesday morning. (I recall that, although none too pleased by the urgency, she seemed to regard this as being 'par for the course'!)

The offences committed by the two boys were comparatively minor and they received conditional discharges. But, all in all, this was something of a 'baptism of fire' for a newly qualified recruit to the service. To my mind it indicated a degree of poor administration on the part of those in charge. However, in fairness to all concerned, there had been something of a time lapse between the departure of my predecessor and my taking up his vacant post. The senior probation officer in charge there had tried his best to 'hold the fort'.

Probation duties of the time summarised

It is worth mentioning here that the range of duties undertaken by probation officers in those far-off days was extensive. In addition to probation supervision (which included children and young persons) officers undertook prison after-care, consent to marry cases, children alleged to be beyond parental control, neighbour quarrels, acting as guardian ad litem in adoption cases, and the attempted resolution of matrimonial disputes. Being just over 23 years of age, I undertook these latter duties with a degree of apprehension. What right did someone of my fairly tender years have to intervene in such matters? As we shall see, a number of these motley duties were eventually passed on to other agencies.

Taking over from my predecessor

My predecessor had decided to emigrate with his family to Australia. I met him very briefly after my interview for the post. It was from him that I learned that the local mental hospital (then called Three Counties) was within my patch (see later). I also learned, much later, that, prior to his decision to emigrate, there had been some serious unpleasantness between himself and his two close Bedford colleagues. The latter had expressed concerns about his professional competence and case handling. Subsequent review of the matter by the Home Office Probation Inspectorate appears to have exonerated him; his two colleagues were mildly criticised for not showing more professional understanding. In addition, my predecessor's departure for the Antipodes had hung in the balance. One of his probationers had been charged with the murder of the latter's wife.

The police had originally wished to call my predecessor as a witness. However, in the event they were satisfied with a detailed written statement and possession of the probation record. The defendant was eventually sent to Broadmoor High Security Hospital. Today such an occurrence would have resulted in a detailed inquiry into the nature and quality of the care and supervision of the case by the service. As I recall, no such inquiry ever took place.

MORE PEOPLE AND PLACES

So, what kind of Probation Service existed in Bedfordshire in 1952? Like a number of other probation service areas it had a small service and, as indicated above, was headed by a senior probation officer (SPO). This was not uncommon. Only the larger areas were headed by principal probation officers (PPOs), later to be designated as chief officers. Moreover, other senior ranks (such as deputy and assistant chiefs) were virtually unknown.

Some of those former principal officers were, at least in my view, 'characters'. Mr. Wolfindin, PPO Liverpool, is said to have claimed to have had close acquaintance with Sigmund Freud (or Frood as he always called him); the PPO in Shropshire (where I had had a practical placement) was an expert bee-keeper and, for reasons I never quite understood, drank copious amounts of milk; 'Jimmy' James, the otherwise highly competent and admired PPO of Hertfordshire, sometimes had problems in making himself clear, as he tended to 'mumble'. Sefton Farmer, PPO London, had at one time been a journalist; he was reputedly able to finish *The Times* crosswords in record time!

During my stay in Bedfordshire I was befriended by Jack Marshall, the PPO in neighbouring Buckinghamshire; he would have liked me to 'defect' to his county. After a good deal of thought I decided not to do so. In those early days there was only one female PPO - Miss Kate Fowler at Sheffield. I never met her, but I gather she was a formidable lady of fairly robust views.

As I have indicated, in the 1950s the Probation Service was small-scale. If you went to a National Association of Probation Officers (NAPO) annual conference, you would most likely know or have heard of a large proportion of those attending. In those early days, principal and other senior grades did not have their own separate organizations. The annual conferences were usually attended by members of the inspectorate.

My 'patch' in Bedfordshire was predominantly rural, but I was based in the Bedford Office. The two other offices were at Luton and Dunstable. My responsibilities were to cover the semi-rural environs of Bedford itself and its northern region (Sharnbrook Division – subsequently abolished). To the south, I covered Biggleswade, which in those days was bisected by the Great North Road (the A1), and I made occasional 'forays' into the Ampthill Division (the area in which the 'Hanratty' killings took place).

The wide geographical spread of my 'patch can be seen by noting its neighbouring county areas - Huntingdonshire (as it then was) and Cambridgeshire. These areas were served by a single probation officer in Huntingdonshire and by just one or two officers in Cambridgeshire. On reflection, I am not altogether sure that it was a good arrangement for these officers to operate in semi-isolation. However, this was mitigated to some extent by the contacts we had established with both services – most notably Cambridgeshire. The Biggleswade Division bordered on Hertfordshire. Here the situation was rather better as Hertfordshire was a fairly large area and was headed by a principal officer 'Jimmy' James (above).

My nearest neighbours were based at Hitchin and I became particularly friendly with Huw Rees (who later left the service to take up a post at the London School of Economics), now sadly deceased. I also enjoyed cordial relationships with the late Fred Jarvis, who became chief officer for Leicester and Leicestershire (so our earlier relationships were re-established when I eventually arrived in Leicester some years later).

I also got to know the late Mark Monger; he too eventually landed up in Leicester where we were both members of staff at the University's School of Social Work (see later). My responsibilities being pretty widespread meant that my monthly mileage claims were not inconsiderable. Even in those far-off, and perhaps less bureaucratic, days they were high. They received intense scrutiny by the ever watchful Mr. Green in the County Treasurer's office. It was not unknown to receive a 'phone call from him querying why one's claim from A to B the previous month differed slightly from the current claim! I often thought that one's explanations – such as traffic diversions due to roadworks – did not entirely convince him!

I should acknowledge here that my Bedford colleagues had slightly mixed views concerning my arrival in Bedfordshire. For one thing I was a 'youngster' - not yet 24 - and I must have seemed a bit of a 'know-all' fresh from training. I think that my brashness must have been something of a cover for my underlying anxieties and uncertainties. My immediate colleagues in the Bedford office were Geoffrey Brunson, who cycled round his Bedford patch as he didn't drive. In those days cycling was not uncommon in urban areas; maybe with the current promotion of 'keep fit', it is having a renaissance.

It may come as something of a surprise to my readers that horseback travel round some patches was also in evidence. One of our older senior colleagues in Hertfordshire was said to have used such means of travel. (I never ascertained whether he got a 'horse allowance'! What I do know, is that a small allowance was paid to my cycling colleague).

My other two close colleagues were Mary Wilkinson, who had been a policewoman in Staffordshire, and Esther Disney, who I worked very happily with as we shared the same petty sessional divisional areas of Biggleswade and Ampthill. I learned much from Esther; I have to say I did not find myself having much in common with my other two colleagues. Mary Wilkinson I considered too much 'old school' and somewhat reactionary. Geoffrey I found a bit 'Olympian' and not very easy to get to know.

I had less contact with my colleagues in the south of the county, but on the occasions I did so, I found them very congenial. Our senior in charge of the service was Eric Basford. He was essentially well-intentioned and humanitarian in his attitudes. However, he was not the best of administrators. Not that he was lazy - far from it, but he always tried to please everybody, and in a managerial position you cannot do that. To his great credit he was very client-centred (to use today's jargon). He persevered with some cases where others had given up. After I had left Bedfordshire the service underwent a degree of re-organization following Home Office Inspection. I was not surprised to learn that Eric (or 'EWB' as he was known in the county) was not considered for the newly created PPO post and an external candidate was appointed. Eric left the county soon afterwards, having been appointed as the principal of the National Children's Home at Frodsham in Cheshire. (I think he had been brought up in the care of the NCH). I learned, somewhat to my surprise, that some years later he had returned to Bedfordshire as a main grade probation officer.

ASPECTS OF PROBATION WORK

As previously stated, my work in a predominantly rural area involved a good deal of travelling. Home visiting sometimes involved going to remote and relatively inaccessible places. Occasionally, Esther Disney and I arranged joint travel, for in truth, Esther was not a very confident driver and tried to avoid it where possible.

My early childhood fear of dogs was reawakened to some degree by encounters with noisy and not always friendly canines. However, I managed to turn these sometimes traumatic experiences to advantage in that, much to my satisfaction, I eventually overcame my fear of dogs. In addition to home visiting, it was also necessary to see clients on their own. To accommodate this it was the practice to hold 'reporting centres' in a few locations. These were conducted in a range of premises such as village and church halls, or county offices such as health centres. Such sessions were not difficult to manage during the light evenings, but in autumn and winter it was a rather different proposition.

I cannot recall actually feeling terribly uneasy or vulnerable during these periods of darkness. However, with hindsight, I can see how 'risky' these encounters could have been. In today's climate of risk obsession I imagine such activities would be strongly disapproved of on health and safety grounds. People sometimes ask me if I was ever assaulted during my work in Bedfordshire. Only once did I come near to it and that involved being seriously threatened by a drunken 'visitor' to the Bedford office where I was the only officer available to deal with him. When I eventually made contact with the local police I was not too pleased to be told 'Oh, he's still with you is he; we've had him here for most of the afternoon and suggested he come to you to see if you could give him a handout'. Co-operation is all very well, but this was stretching it somewhat!

Our best work was often done in collaboration and co-operation with colleagues in other agencies. These were, and still should be, essential ingredients of successful probation work. However today, the complex arrangements for such collaboration, and the increasing complexity of the problems dealt with, sometimes make such co-operation less productive than it might be.

Inspection

In those days our work was the subject of regular inspections by the Home Office Probation Inspectorate. In my first years as a probation officer I was inspected three times; all of these were enjoyable and instructive experiences.

Newly appointed entrants were given a preliminary inspection after about three months. Mine was conducted by the genial but not easily fooled Mr. Rocksborough-Smith. I learned subsequent to his visit that he deemed me to have settled in well, even though two of my Bedford colleagues still viewed me with a degree of reserve. Then, at twelve months, came a further and more comprehensive examination of one's work. This was in order for a newly appointed officer to be confirmed in his or her post, the first year being a probationary period. (Such 'confirmation inspections' were subsequently superceded by 'in-house' inspection and approval). My confirmation inspection was undertaken by Mr. Ralph Beeson, the deputy chief inspector. To my relief he gave me a good report and I was duly confirmed.

My third experience of inspection was as part of a general routine inspection of the whole local service. Our general inspection was carried out by Mr. Harold Morton, again a genial but highly perceptive inspector. In later years he became a valued close colleague and family friend. During inspections it was customary for the inspectors to meet local officials such as clerks to the justices and members of the (then) Probation Committee (particularly the chairman). This was in addition to a general presentation by the inspector(s) to members of the whole committee.

On the occasion of Harold Morton's visit he wished to see the clerk to the justices at Biggleswade - some 12 miles away from the Bedford office. I was asked to chauffeur him. Harold Morton was a *very* tall chap, some six feet six, and large framed as well. In those days my car was an elderly two-seater 1935 Morris tourer. Getting him into the confines of my vehicle was no mean feat, but we managed it!

Working with the local bench

Clerks to the court were key figures affecting the success or otherwise of our work. Our clerk at Biggleswade was a Mr. Clough-Waters. I found him a somewhat difficult man to relate to. On some occasions he could be very charming and helpful, at others distant and irritable. (I sometimes wondered if he suffered from bouts of poor health).

Fortunately, most of my dealings were with his excellent and supportive assistant, Miss Syvyer. She was unfailingly helpful and kind. The clerk at Sharnbrook in the north of the county was the elderly Mr. E. T. Williams. He had all the qualities of a Dickensian gentleman (in the best meaning of that word). He was a non-driver, so on the fairly infrequent occasions that I was required to attend at Sharnbrook, either I or Miss Wilkinson would provide a taxi service for him and his assistant – Miss Fulger. His old-world dignity tended to make his approach to his work somewhat anachronistic. If he thought I might have something to offer the court concerning possible disposal he would say 'Mr. Prins, have you been retained in this matter?', much as he would ask a defending solicitor. My services were not required often, partly because the court only 'sat' about once a month, but mainly because the chairman - retired Air Commodore Higgins - hadn't much time for non-custodial sentences.

Sharnbrook court formed part of the police station. In winter, a roaring fire made the court room very hot and stuffy. On one occasion our regular prosecuting officer - Inspector Dennis - nearly singed the seat of his trousers!

The clerk at Ampthill was also called Williams. He was a

comparatively young man. I did not get to know him at all well as I only attended Ampthill infrequently. But I did come to regard the chairman of the bench at Ampthill – Mr. Owen – as a very forward-looking and thoughtful magistrate, a view shared by my colleague Esther Disney.

And what of the rest of the magistracy? They were drawn from a predominantly rural community. My main bench was at Biggleswade, presided over by the wise and benign Henry Chapman - a barrister by training, but non-practising; he was a businessman. His deputy was Mr. John Fisher, who ran the local hardware store in Biggleswade town square. Other members of the Bench included Colonel Bowes-Lyon - uncle to the late Queen Mother - and one or two local women-folk. In those far-off days it would have been considered a pretty representative bench. Formal training for the magistracy was of course then pretty well non-existent!

The police and the higher courts

As to the police, most of one's dealings with them were in their then role as prosecutors. Only very rarely in those days did the police brief solicitors or counsel. Chief inspector Norman normally prosecuted at Biggleswade. He was a man well disposed towards the probation service and was a shrewd observer of human behaviour (and misbehaviour). It was his custom to telephone me prior to the regular Wednesday sitting of the court to warn me that I might be needed.

Occasionally his place would be taken by the area superintendent – 'Dick' Morgan – subsequently to be involved in the early investigation of the 'A6 murder' near Ampthill.

Attendance by probation officers at the then Assizes and Quarter Sessions (replaced by the Crown Court in 1972) were, of course, less frequent. The opening of the assize was an opportunity for public display and acclamation. Following the customary church service, the retinue would process to the court (in our case to County Hall where it was held). The procession was headed by the 'red' judge with his traditional nosegay of sweet-smelling herbs; this bore witness to the days when the smell of bodily secretions and the threat of the dreaded plague were regular phenomena.

The judge would be followed by his retinue; this included his page, the bestockinged High Sheriff and local dignitaries. The judges' reputations went before them. Some had a reputation for severity and rigidly enforced decorum, the late Mr. Justice Croome-Johnson being an example of someone with such an attitude. I thought him a somewhat ill-tempered man. He would become very angry if anyone 'muttered' or moved during oath-taking; he would sternly halt the proceedings and threaten the offender with contempt of court.

By way of a contrast, a much more mellow and humane approach was offered by Mr. Justice Finnemore. Most were keen to expedite the task of 'gaol delivery' (a main purpose of the assize being not only to punish wrong-doing, but to empty the gaols of those awaiting trial). Such a function was espoused with enthusiasm by the late Lord Chief Justice, Rayner Goddard. He would occasionally 'sally forth' from the High Court in London and conduct proceedings with great despatch. Although some considered him a somewhat harsh sentencer, he could also demonstrate a humane awareness of human frailty. Those who presided over the second-tier courts - Quarter Sessions - sat either as 'chairman' in the county areas and as 'recorders' in the Boroughs.

Occasionally, one would come across unprofessional conduct in such office holders. The chairman of our County Sessions and Recorder of Bedford – the late Charles Lammond Henderson, QC - was an example of such behaviour. For reasons which I could never fathom, he seemed to take singular pleasure in belittling many of the professionals who had the misfortune to appear before him, be they members of the Bar, the police, psychiatrists, prison medical officers or the Probation Service. As a result of our own sense of concern at being treated in this way, we brought our worries to the notice of the County Probation Committee. I recall that they held some form of inquiry at which we were asked to give evidence. The committee must have considered our complaints to be legitimate since they did not re-appoint him when his term of office expired. However, he did remain as Recorder for the Borough of Bedford. Over the years I have worked with members of the Bar and all levels of the judiciary. I have always found them to be courteous, considerate and humane. Sadly, Charles Henderson seems to have been a notable exception.

Working with the local 'asylum'

I noted earlier that the local mental hospital ('asylum' in those far-off days) was located within my patch. Three Counties, as it was then called (subsequently known as Fairfield Hospital), was a large Victorian edifice, in a secluded spot at the end of a long winding drive. Structurally and in location, it was not markedly different from many similar institutions of that era. It is perhaps no coincidence that it was located in the sprawling village of Arlesey, the latter rumoured to contain a number of products of incestuous relationships. However, I never found any evidence to substantiate such rumours, though those folk I came across did seem to live rather in a world of their own.

As also indicated earlier, the Criminal Justice Act of 1948 enabled courts to make probation orders with a requirement for mental treatment. Those placed under such orders as in-patients were subject to management by the medical and other staff. In those days the probation officer's remit was largely confined to making arrangements for the discharge or amendment of such orders. This somewhat limited intervention could of course be over-ridden by agreement for more active co-operation between the medical staff and the probation officer dealing with the case.

Over time, this type of 'interventive' relationship developed and such orders are now part of a large menu of community type orders.

Having been encouraged to go beyond my somewhat legally restricted role, I became increasingly interested in the relationship between various forms of mental disorder and criminality. At the time there were no designated forensic psychiatrists as such. Of course many psychiatrists had taken an interest in criminal behaviour, for example Henry Maudsley, Norwood East (Prison Medical Service), the psychoanalysts Melitta Schmideberg and Edward Glover, and the child psychiatrists Donald Winnicott and Emanuel Miller - to name but a few.

Developing links with local psychiatrists continued to foster my interest in this relationship and so, after nearly five years in Bedfordshire,[1] I decided it was time to continue my professional education. With a degree of encouragement from the ever-helpful Harold Morton of the inspectorate (but alas no offer of funding), I applied to undertake the Mental Health Course at the London School of Economics, one of the few centres in those days where people could train as a psychiatric social worker (PSW).[2]

---

1. Two well-known people are historically associated with Bedfordshire. John Bunyan (1628-88) was born in Bedford and spent most of his life in the county. He spent several years in Bedford Gaol, where he wrote both parts of his most famous work, *Pilgrim's Progress* (1684). John Howard became High Sheriff of Bedford in 1773. His contacts with prisoners in Bedford Gaol led him to travel widely and inquire into the conditions under which prisoners, in England and abroad, were held. This resulted in his classic work, *The State of The Prisons* (1777). The present day Howard League For Penal Reform bears his name.

2. Each Petty Sessional Division (PSD) (as they then were) had to form a 'Case Committee', from representatives of the petty sessional magistracy. Their task was two-fold. First, to have a general oversight of our supervisory efforts, and second to offer support for our endeavours. I always considered that these two *desiderata* could be in conflict. The degree to which committee members could advise on case management was somewhat limited, and might be seen in some instances as interference in matters of professional judgement and confidentiality, especially as some committees asked to be provided with written summaries of our efforts.

CHAPTER FOUR

A Productive Year at the LSE

I had some anxieties about applying for the one-year Mental Health Course at the London School of Economics (LSE). This was partly because I knew that it was not an easy course on which to gain acceptance, and partly because I wasn't sure how I might fund myself. At that time, the Home Office tended to prefer to sponsor officers on the Advanced Casework Course at the Tavistock Clinic in London, with its well-regarded psycho-analytic orientation. However, had Home Office sponsorship been available to me, I'm not sure I would have accepted it. At that time, I was uncertain that I would wish to return to the Probation Service. Fortunately, I discovered that the Department of Health would sponsor students on the course provided that they were prepared to accept two years' employment in a recognized National Health Service centre. I was happy to accept such conditions.

THE SELECTION PROCESS

The selection process consisted of a detailed formal written application, the nomination of two referees, and two interviews with staff members associated with the course - one an academic tutor and the other a fieldwork supervisor. Both interviews were pretty searching, but in no way unpleasant. I was an anxious interviewee and had real doubts as to whether or not I would be accepted on the course. Somewhat to my surprise, the outcome was positive. I learned subsequently that a senior member of the Probation Service (the late Doris Sullivan, later an assistant chief probation officer in London) had acquitted herself with distinction on the course, and that maybe the course staff had come to the conclusion that having a member of the Probation Service had its merits! (Doris, who I and my wife later got to know very well, gained a distinction, setting me a somewhat daunting precedent). The course was headed by the late Kay McDougall, a knowledge-able psychiatric social worker who 'operated' with a great deal of friendly informality. Our other tutors were Joan Smith (later Joan Hutton) and 'Reg' Wright, who subsequently went on to work as a senior member of staff at the (then) Central Council for Education and Training in Social Work.

THE COURSE

They all contributed to the core teaching. Outside lecturers - from the Maudsley Hospital and elsewhere - covered specialist topics such as neurology, psychopathology, mental deficiency (as it was then called) and aspects of social psychology. There were also seminars in social casework practice - at which towards the end of the course, we had to present a dissertation. (I recall that, perhaps not surprisingly, I chose the topic of Authority in Casework!).

The course was intensive, stressful, but ultimately highly rewarding. Two practical placements had to be undertaken, one in an adult setting and the other in child guidance, as it was then called. For my first placement I found myself at the Adult Department of the Maudsley Hospital. (Maudsley was, and still is, regarded as one of the 'top' centres in psychiatry in the UK). Margaret Eden was the senior psychiatric social worker in charge. She had succeeded Elizabeth Howarth, who had a reputation as being somewhat formidable. She had left the Maudsley to oversee a project in Shoreditch. She subsequently became a colleague when I worked at the (then) North West London Polytechnic (see later). My supervisor was Irene Lissman. I found her rather intimidating (a bit like Miss Gruber of the FWA: see *Chapter 2*), and her concepts difficult to comprehend. To be frank, I didn't enjoy the experience or feel I had gained that much from it. To be fair, I don't think she found me an easy student to supervise. To make matters more uncomfortable, she had failed a fellow student in her current placement, and I think this impacted on the group of us who were at the Maudsley as a whole.

We were allowed to 'sit in' on out-patient clinics run by the likes of Dr Kraupl Taylor, Dr Linford Rees (later Professor at St. Bartholomew's), and the late Dr Felix Post, the distinguished psycho-geriatrician. I also renewed my acquaintance with the late Edgar Myers. I had first met him when he accompanied a very difficult client of his to an appearance at Biggleswade Magistrates' Court. He was a very perceptive and well informed psychiatric social worker with a considerable interest in psychopathy. He subsequently joined the academic staff at the London School of Economics and later became our external examiner at the Psychiatric Social Work Course at Leeds University (*Chapter 9*).

At the time I was a student at the Maudsley it was presided over by the late Sir Aubrey Lewis. He had a somewhat fearsome reputation.

As students, we were expected to present a 'case' at the Wednesday afternoon Case Conferences at the nearby St. Francis Hospital (an observation centre for acute cases). Somewhat to my relief, when the time came for me to take my 'turn' at this, Sir Aubrey was away, and the conference was taken by Dr Michael Shepherd (later to become Professor). I survived the experience, but I found Dr Shepherd somewhat remote and not a little patronising. Miss Lissman rated me as an 'average' student (and I guess I rated her as an 'average' supervisor'!). For all the learning advantages, I wasn't sorry to say farewell to the Maudsley, despite an invitation from Margaret Eden to apply for a post at the end of my course. One of the inducements held out to me was the opportunity to work with Dr Peter Scott in his forensic out-patients clinic. As I show in the following chapter, a chance development in my career provided me with an excellent opportunity to work with him.

My final placement was at the Child Guidance Clinic at St. George's Hospital, Hyde Park (where by happy co-incidence - or design by my tutors - my fiancée was a nurse). My supervisor at St. George's was Clemency Chapman, who I found to be a congenial teacher and subsequently a good friend. The clinic was well known and respected, the senior psychiatric social worker being Mrs. Elizabeth Edkins, and the other social worker Miss Sally Hornby. The clinical director was the eminent child psychiatrist, Dr Emmanuel Miller. He was Jonathan Miller's father and his mother was the novelist Betty Miller. With two such well-known and respected parents, it is hardly surprising that Jonathan (now Sir Jonathan) developed his polymathic abilities.

During my period at St. George's, I learned much about developmental child psychology and psychiatry. Dr. Miller was a very 'available' teacher, as were his colleagues.

THE OUTCOME

I think my supervisor had recognized quite early that I had suffered a blow to my self-confidence at the Maudsley. She was highly supportive of my developing abilities as a psychiatric social worker.

My immediate predecessor at the clinic had been Doris Sullivan - referred to earlier - and I felt I had to follow in her distinguished footsteps. I did well in the final examinations, and much to my surprise passed with distinction and headed the pass list. Sometimes success seems to come when you are least expecting it to.

CHAPTER FIVE

Boys on Remand

I fulfilled my obligation to the Department of Health by securing a post as a psychiatric social worker at the [then] Stamford House Remand Home for Boys. (Later it was also to function as an approved school classifying centre). I worked at Stamford House from 1957 until 1959. It was run under the control of the [then] London County Council (LCC). It was Doris Sullivan who had alerted me to the possibilities of a post, as she had had her last practical placement there.

A DUAL PURPOSE FACILITY

The vacancy was an additional one, but a further post had also arisen due to the departure of the current holder to work in Canada. This post was subsequently filled by Sarah Nairn who, like Clemency Chapman, became our firm friend (and attended our wedding).

My interview for the post was essentially a comfortable one, but also quite searching. As I recall, the members of the interviewing panel were the acting superintendent of the home – Mr. John O'Hare, Doctor Scott and an LCC representative. Subsequently, John Burns, a senior child care worker in Bristol, was appointed as director. Stamford House was located in London's Goldhawk Road and served the Metropolitan Juvenile Court area. Very occasionally it also served one or two courts in the Home Counties. This latter service was provided in particularly difficult cases, the request usually being for 'Doctor Scott to provide a report in this case please', such was his reputation in assessing juvenile as well as adult offenders.

When, in 1958, the remand home provided the approved school assessment service referred to above, its intake of new residents was high - and sometimes there were well over a hundred boys awaiting assessment and or the disposal of their case.

One consultant and two senior registrars (as they were then called) attended regularly and registrars in training came for varying periods. The senior registrars included such noted figures as Donald West (later Professor at the Institute of Criminology at Cambridge), and the late Professor Sula Wolff – the well-known child psychiatrist. There was a 'sister' centre for girls at neighbouring Cumberlow Lodge. The senior consultant there was the late Doctor (Professor) Trevor Gibbens. At Stamford House there were two full-time educational psychologists and a very experienced visiting and insightful general practitioner ('Chick' Carter).

Working under pressure

Most of our work was carried out under considerable pressure, as the timescale for the preparation of reports was usually three weeks or less. I found that courts referred the boys for a variety of reasons. For example, the number of offences they had committed, the unusual nature of an offence, or because the probation officer and the magistrates were simply baffled by the youngster's behaviour.

I once took a sample of 120 boys remanded for psychiatric examination between January and November, 1958. I discovered that the number of their previous offences, as admitted by them or proved by evidence was as set out in the chart overleaf.[1]

---

1. Prins, 1959 and 1961.

No previous offence	35
One such offence	40
Two previous offences	28
Three such offences	11
Four or more	6
Total	120

The number of first offenders may seem high, but most of these had a prolonged history of other behavioural disturbances, whether before, or associated with, their current offence. The number of boys with one previous conviction suggested that it was at a second court appearance that the court tended to seek further advice. Very occasionally we were asked to see a small number of boys on bail. As a team we considered that this was a useful practice that could have been used more frequently.

Linked with, and ideally inseparable from, our court report functions we provided a secondary (but no less important) diagnostic and advisory service for probation officers and occasionally other workers in cases involving special difficulty. In this way I got to know many members of the London Probation Service and other neighbouring services. The pressure involved in providing comprehensive reports in the short time referred to above was considerable. For example, in any one week we might have prepared some thirty or more reports. Our task as psychiatric social workers was largely to take a full 'social history' from the boys' parents or guardians. This is not to diminish in any way the excellent reports provided for us by probation officers, but our information was sought to amplify these officers' inquiries. Time, and sometimes distance, precluded home visiting.

DEALING WITH PARENTS

Some of the views expressed by the parents or guardians were revealing. Our letters to parents soliciting help sometimes produced surprising and very helpful results. One mother, who lived in the north of England, replied that she was 'not much good on paper' and took the train south to see us. In this case (and in a number of others) the interview was extremely helpful. I learned that she had had a very difficult deprived childhood and continually tried to off-set the father's alleged over-strict attitudes by her extreme over-indulgence. In the face of such conflicting attitudes it was not surprising their son's behaviour was based upon conflicting and anxiety-producing expectations.

Our basic task was to assess the parental attitude to the boy and his offence. Our history taking was essentially similar to that undertaken in a non-forensic child guidance clinic, the main exception being that our interviews had to be carried out in a 'one-off' situation instead of developing over several. This tended inevitably to overload the interview with fact finding. The probation report often only provided a modest account of developmental history. In our interviews missing clues could often be discerned.

One lad had been remanded for report for what seemed to be a baffling pattern of truancy. Careful and sensitive inquiry revealed that 'dad' was not dad at all. The lad had suspected this for some time, but mother had missed some of the warning signs – 'Dad and I don't look much alike do we …?' In another case, a boy had been referred to us because of cycle stealing. Superficially, the home seemed stable enough, but a detailed social history revealed that his birth had not only been unwanted (he was illegitimate), but precipitate and he had received a head injury that had resulted in fits. The mother's guilt over his conception had led to over-indulgence which brought about frequent rows with her husband over the latter's disciplinary measures.

Parents needed sympathetic responses. They sometimes presented a very hostile attitude towards the courts and their staff. Such attitudes were, for the most part, born of their own adverse experiences of parental handling. Such parents had often had deprived childhoods. Mrs. 'A's parents separated after a good many years of quarrelling. Her mother always belittled her in front of her siblings and when the marriage finally broke up Mrs. 'A' was sent to a children's home. She was thoroughly unhappy there. Eventually she went into 'service'. While still a very young girl she found herself pregnant by the man she subsequently married. He was an irresponsible and feckless individual who had left his wife to cope unaided. With their large family she became increasingly despondent and soon acquired a reputation as an inadequate and incompetent mother. It became clear in my long interview with her that what she needed was someone who could recognize and accept her feelings of inadequacy, yet give her some encouragement for the good efforts she made. This seemed to have been a very helpful experience for her and she was able to talk about her experiences and her relationship with her mother. A subsequent conversation (and with Mrs. 'A's consent) with the probation officer involved in the case enabled him to gain a greater understanding of her current behaviour.

... AND LEARNING ABOUT DELINQUENCY

During this time I learned a good deal more about the genesis of persistent delinquency in boys. In particular, the need to take a detailed longitudinal view of youthful misbehaviour. The experience at Stamford House had also helped me to 'hone' my casework skills. As already stated, not only did one have to gain information about family background and attitudes, but all of this within a very limited timescale and without leaving a parent or parents feeling that they may have said too much so as to leave themselves emotionally exposed. One also had to acknowledge and deal with one's own hostile feelings towards such parents who had shown themselves to be anti-social, feckless and occasionally abusive to their children. It was essential to try to deal with one's angry and un-empathic feelings if one was going to engender a helpful response. It was a skill I tried to develop during my time at Stamford House, and which was to prove most useful in some of my later work as an educator and facilitator of others.

LEAVING STAMFORD HOUSE

I decided to leave Stamford House for three reasons. First, I had fulfilled my obligations for the grant aid I had received. Second, being recently married, I sought to find occupation somewhat nearer to our home in Harrow. Third, I felt I needed to return (at least for a short time) to opportunities for more long-term casework. In following a dictum of my late mother-in-law that 'There's nothing for the dumb', I wrote a letter of inquiry to the late William (Bill) Todd, then the principal probation officer for Middlesex, enquiring after the possibilities of work in the area. I received a highly encouraging response and, following a formal interview, but not one as traumatic as my interview in Bedfordshire (see *Chapter 3*), I was assigned to Hendon Magistrates' Court. Happily, this was within easy distance of home.

CHAPTER SIX

Probation Revisited

Hendon Magistrates' Court covered a comparatively large area of North-West London. It is proximate to Harrow in one direction and Cricklewood in the other (later to be the location for the serial killer Dennis Nilsen's nefarious killings). The Probation Service was housed in a prefabricated building adjacent to the Court House. Our offices could become stiflingly hot in summer and very cold in winter. However, their proximity to the court saved time and energy otherwise spent in travel! Concerning travel, my two closest colleagues, Kate Flood (as she then was) and Ralph Stephen shared our use of the 'County Car' (a somewhat 'tired' Ford Anglia). The Probation Committee had agreed that this vehicle would be stationed at our house, since my colleagues and I lived reasonably near each other.

My other colleagues were Tom Illingworth, Wilf Burnip, Fred Crainer and Judith Kennedy – a congenial group. (They did not seem to have had the reservations about my competence expressed by some of my former colleagues at the Bedford Probation Office!). In fact, one or two of them appeared to be a bit in awe of me. Having trained as a psychiatric social worker, they tended to think that I would have the answers to many of the 'imponderables' that arose in our caseloads. They quickly learned that 'idols have feet of clay'!

Our senior probation officer, Sid Thorne, managed us with much friendly forbearance and wisdom. We became close to the Thorne family, and their two sons (Jeremy and David) became like older 'sibs' to our two young children. David eventually followed us to Leeds (see *Chapter 9*) as a medical student. There he subsequently met and married Jane, who was a nurse at the

Leeds Infirmary. Their wedding, which we attended, took place in idyllic surroundings in rural Norfolk.

The work at Hendon was in sharp contrast to that of rural Bedfordshire. However, the problems presented by the clients ('service consumers' in today's parlance) were similar. Proximity to our clients made contact easier than that existing in a rural setting. The magistrates' court at Hendon was presided over by Mr. 'Tommy' Graham. He had a particular antipathy to shop-lifters (of which admittedly there were far too many in our area); first offenders might well receive a prison sentence unless there were substantial mitigating circumstances. We were fortunate that the clerk to the justices was Oswald Cargill; he took a keen interest in criminological and psychiatric matters. Sometimes we wondered why he had not trained as a probation officer!

Attendance at the higher courts (the Old Bailey and the Middlesex Sessions) was not a frequent occurrence. I recall the sessions at that time were presided over by Ewan Montague QC, who had had a distinguished record in the Second World War; and, if I remember rightly, was involved in the film 'The Man Who Never Was', being played by the actor the late Clifton Webb.

AWAKENING AN INTEREST IN TEACHING

Our work in Middlesex was subject to regular inspection by a member of the headquarters staff, in my case by Mr. Henden Cole, the assistant chief probation officer. By a somewhat strange coincidence I had met Mr. Cole when I was a child, since he and my father had been involved in a prison after-care project. As already stated, my colleagues and the hierarchy seemed to have somewhat unrealistic expectation of my potential as a 'trainer' - to the extent that they encouraged me to apply for the newly created post of assistant chief probation officer with responsibility for training. There were four candidates for the post including myself.

Interviews in the morning were before the whole Committee (shades of my Bedford experience!); following these, three of us were called back for interview by a sub-committee in the afternoon. Not altogether to my surprise, I did not get the job; it went to a much better qualified candidate – Adam McGillivray – who was highly successful in the post, eventually becoming principal probation officer when 'Bill' Todd retired.

Looking back, I think that the seeds of an interest in training had been sown by the encouragement I had received at Hendon. In addition, during my time at Stamford House, I had been invited to apply for an assistant lecturer post at the London School of Economics (LSE) to teach on the Mental Health Course. I duly did so. The interview was a relaxed experience. The chair was taken by Professor Carr-Saunders – the school's director. The other members of the panel were Kay MacDougall and another senior member of the academic staff. Two of us had applied, my fellow candidate being Tony Forder, who was appointed. I was told informally that 'he had obtained the post because he had considerable experience as a field-work supervisor, but that on all other counts I would have been an acceptable candidate'

BACK TO HENDON . . .

To return to Hendon. My nascent interest in training had been fuelled further by being asked to supervise a Home Office probation student in his final placement. The student in question was Michael Day (who happened to live locally). Fortunately, somewhat by way of contrast to his first placement, our experience was a thoroughly congenial and productive one and well received by the inspectorate. (During this period I had also been asked to take some casework seminars for the Home Office Probation Course). Michael subsequently demonstrated his considerable qualities by gaining rapid promotion through the probation hierarchy, eventually serving as chief probation officer for the West Midlands, and latterly as chair of the (then) Commission for Racial Equality, and being knighted for his services.

It is not surprising, as a result of my experiences in Middlesex, that I decided I should seek to enter the academic world of social work education. I saw the post of assistant lecturer advertised at the North-West London Polytechnic and applied for it.

CHAPTER SEVEN

A Stint in Further Education

The North-West London Polytechnic was located in Kentish Town. Its work and ethos concerned themselves with a wide range of further educational activities - living up to its name 'Polytechnic'. Subsequently it received (as did many others) university status. Although in many ways this 'promotion' in educational status had many benefits, I think the transition 'dumbed down' (to use the current 'in words') the excellent work that such institutions did with their vocational orientation. In my opinion, the political view that fifty per cent of young people should receive a university education has proved to be a mixed blessing.

Training for a trade has tended to be denigrated and, as a consequence, pride in such work has been diminished. One might well ask, where are our cohorts of skilled artisans (such as plumbers, 'brickies' and carpenters)? A qualification for such employment used to be prized and eagerly sought after. The term 'apprentice' now tends to be seen as the outcome of jumping through Lord Alan Sugar's many hoops!

SOCIAL STUDIES

An important aspect of the polytechnic's work was its Department of Social Studies. The advertisement for the post for which I applied indicated that the work would consist mainly of assisting with the training of residential childcare staff. As the advertisement did not specify that residential child-care experience was a prerequisite, I was not put off applying for the post. I thought that my spell at Stamford House would be viewed favourably by the interview panel, and indeed this was the case. I recall that the interview panel consisted of Mr. Saunders Harris - the college principal, the head of department – Miss Anderson, and Miss Clement-Brown, the Home Office Children's Department inspector in charge of child care training.

My reservations concerning the wisdom of applying for the post were subsequently borne out. Miss Bremner, the tutor in charge of the course, quickly made known to me her disappointment that someone without residential child care experience had been appointed. This disappointment tended to colour our working relationship, though I have to say she was not an unpleasant colleague. I surmised that the polytechnic wanted to inject a slightly broader element into the course. In addition, the somewhat politically incorrect view was, I guess, that it would be no bad thing to have appointed a young male member of staff in what was predominantly a department staffed by women. In the event, I managed to cope with the limited academic input required, and I found my tutorial visits to the students placed in a wide range of childcare establishments most rewarding. (I'm not so sure that the students I visited obtained value for money).

WIDER SOCIAL WORK PRACTICE

As time went by, I felt I needed experience that focused rather more upon a wider range of social work practice. Fate came to my aid. The late nineteen-fifties and early nineteen-sixties witnessed the development of formal training arrangements for those engaged in local authority social welfare work. The focus in those early days was largely on existing 'mature' social work staff. This occurred as a result of a report by Eileen Younghusband's Committee on the need for such training. In those far-off days the name of Eileen Younghusband was perhaps not as well known as it was to become subsequently. (She was a descendant of the explorer Sir Francis Younghusband). Her lack of 'fame' at that time meant that we received some rather curious requests from aspiring candidates. One wrote in seeking details for 'your training for "young husbands"'. Perhaps we missed out on a golden opportunity!

The polytechnic had advertised for an assistant lecturer to work alongside the lecturer in charge of the course. I duly applied for the post (I think much to Miss Bremner's relief). The formal interview for the post was pretty searching; the panel member I remember best was Dame Eileen herself. One of my duties was going to be to teach a course in social history. I had studied the subject under the skilful guidance of Dr Peter Kingsford on my social science course but, inevitably, it was a somewhat sketchy account. When Dame Eileen (as she had become) asked me how I would teach such a course I told her that I would take a developmental (sequential) approach. She rather threw me by asking if I had not considered working from the present and going backwards!

Despite this difference of view I got the job, and my senior colleague was to be Joan Vann - a congenial co-worker. She subsequently left the college to join the Department of Health and Social Services Inspectorate. Soon after the Younghusband course, it was decided to set up a similar course for childcare fieldwork staff. The late Elizabeth Howarth was appointed. As mentioned in *Chapter 4*, she had headed up the training element in the Social Work Department at the Maudsley Hospital. She was subsequently involved in an interesting experimental project in Shoreditch. She came to us with a somewhat formidable reputation and her views on social work training were not entirely in accord with those of Joan Vann. Because of this, the atmosphere was somewhat tense at times.

To make matters worse, she was an inveterate chain smoker and this did not endear her to some of her colleagues. Had she been alive today she would have found her work-place 'habit' unlawful. Amidst all this 'hassle' I often found myself as an uncomfortable 'pig in the middle'. Once again, fate came to my rescue. During my time at the polytechnic I had been broadening my interest, particularly in the fields of forensic mental health and criminality. I had become a member of the Education Committee of the (then) Institute For the Study and Treatment of Delinquency (ISTD)[1] - a committee serviced by the admirable late Eve Saville, who managed the affairs of the institute with a single-handed devotion to duty.

OUTSIDE INVOLVEMENTS

I also served on the Executive Committee of the Howard League for Penal Reform. I became acquainted with a very interesting range of people. As I recall, the committee was chaired by the late Sir George Benson, and the league's secretary in those days was Hugh Klare, well known as a penal reformer. Other members included the elderly child psychiatrist, Marjorie Franklin. She usually arrived late for meetings and caused a great 'stir' until she was comfortably seated!

I had also been asked to serve as an 'independent' member of a small committee set up by the (then) National Association of Discharged Prisoners' Aid Societies (NADPAS). This concerned itself with the selection and appointment of prison welfare officers. The work of NADPAS was later taken over by the newly formed National Association for the Care and Resettlement of Offenders (Nacro); eventually seconded members of the Probation Service took over as prison probation officers. During those years there was a move to develop a 'joined up' Prison and Probation Service – a foretaste of what was to become in more recent times the National Offender Management Service (NOMS), demonstrating that there's not much new under the sun! (During my time in the

---

1. The forerunner of the Centre for Crime and Justice Studies (CCJS).

Home Office there was much debate about such a proposal as noted further in *Chapter 8*).

PROBATION INSPECTOR

But perhaps of greater importance in relation to my future career was a request from the Probation Inspectorate to undertake social casework seminars at the Probation Training Centre at Rainer House. I enjoyed this aspect of my extra-mural work enormously in what was to become an increasingly conducive environment. The inspectorate wished to expand its complement of training inspectors (now headed by May Irvine). She had been a very experienced psychiatric social worker in the Department of Psychiatry at Manchester University, and concerned with a training course for PSWs. It was suggested to me in a most circumspect fashion that I might wish to consider applying for one of the two new posts being advertised. I use the word circumspect advisedly, since any hint of 'canvassing' for what were established Civil Service posts would have been deemed quite improper. The issue was minimally resolved by my being sent, anonymously, a very small newspaper cutting containing the advertisement! As I deemed myself to be qualified to apply, it seemed to my wife and I that it could be a good career move were I to be successful.

Candidates for what were regarded as fairly senior central government appointments were required to be interviewed by a Selection Committee chaired by a Civil Service Commissioner. The interview was relaxed in nature. In addition to the chair, the other members of the board were the principal probation inspector, Finlay Macrae ('Mac' as he was known by everyone: see *Chapter 8*), Mrs. Kay McDougall, who had been one of my tutors at the LSE, and a representative of the Establishment Division of the Home Office. (Some years earlier I had applied unsuccessfully for a post as an inspector in the Home Office Children's

Inspectorate. This was not such a happy interview experience. On reflection, I was quite ill-advised to make such an application). In due course a cyclostyled note arrived informing me that I and a fellow candidate, Joan Shepherd, had been successful in the 'competition'.

This somewhat laconic communication was followed up by more detailed and personalised material setting out the preliminary requirements before a formal offer of appointment could be made. These included a medical, criminal records check and various other matters. Once these had been concluded to the satisfaction of the commission, the latter would issue what was then known as a 'Certificate of Qualification' enabling the candidate to take up the post. And so, in May 1962, I took up my duties as a probation inspector. My colleague to be, Joan Shepherd, arrived shortly afterwards and the two of us became firm friends and a bit like lost souls in the somewhat unfamiliar environment of a central government department.

CHAPTER EIGHT

Not Always an 'Obedient' or 'Civil' Servant

The Home Office is an ancient Department of State, having been established as long ago as 1782. At various times in its history it has dealt with wild birds, anatomy regulations, dangerous dogs, drugs, the exercise of the Royal Prerogative of Mercy and, of course, the protection of the public through its oversight of criminal justice matters. A number of these aspects of its work have, at various times, been re-allocated to other central government departments, such as the Department of Health. Modern-day events (particularly during the years 2006-2007) led the (then) Home Secretary - Dr John Reid - to declare the department as being 'unfit for purpose' – a panic statement fuelled by media concerns about illegal immigrants and absconding or depredations of a small handful of recently released prisoners on supervision in the community.

A SPRAWLING ROLE

The department certainly carried a range of somewhat disparate obligations; I believe it has been described over the years as a 'residual legatee'. In view of these many activities, its current functions have now been split mainly between two departments - the Ministry of Justice (with responsibility for prisons and probation) and the Home Office (with responsibility for policing and security).[1] It is difficult to discern with any degree of accuracy what

---

1. The Ministry of Justice also has a wide range of justice-related and constitutional functions. The reduced Home Office is sometimes described as 'slimmed down'.

this 'split' is achieving in the exercise of its functions. A friend of mine in the newly designated Ministry of Justice commented to me with wry detachment – 'same work, same computer, just different headed paper'. The impression I gained was that the workload was no less onerous.

Before my own appointment to the Home Office, I had very little knowledge of the range of its activities and the manner in which these were carried out. I was soon to learn some of the finer implications concerning such matters. As a permanent employee (though classed as a 'professional civil servant' with membership of the Institute of Professional Civil Servants' (IPCS)) one's 'extra-mural' activities were quite severely restricted if they were considered likely to cause potential embarrassment to the department. For example, the acceptance of even very small gifts from grateful students was prohibited.

I recall being offered a splendidly ornate cane (walking stick) by one of our overseas students at the end of his course. I was not permitted to accept, the reason given by my boss was that 'who was to say: we might perhaps be at war with the student's country of origin at some date in the future'!

Coping with the close restrictions on civil servants

Professional writing at the request of external bodies was also not encouraged. I had been asked to write a review of a criminological work, but had to refuse the invitation. Some months later a request arrived from a journal in the United States for a paper to be written on 'Aspects of Probation Training in England and Wales'. I was asked to undertake the task, I think as a kind of compensation for not being allowed to undertake the book review. The paper (after much revision by my superiors) eventually saw the 'light of day' in the *Federal Probation Journal*.

Such scrutiny and amendment by the Home Office hierarchy was initially difficult to become accustomed to, especially for someone who had been engaged in academic writing for some time. Some of the restrictions operated under the aegis of the Official Secrets Act which, strictly speaking, operates for life, but the effects of which are now much less onerous in practice, so that professional civil servants are now much more free to write and lecture.

'Pressing', 'immediate' and 'urgent'

The administrative work of the department as a whole was largely processed through the passing of memos contained in files of varying length. They were labelled in accordance with the immediacy of the response required. I recall that 'Pressing' merited a yellow tag, ' Immediate' and 'Urgent' red ones.

Folklore had it that the most important label of all was that bearing the title 'Sentence of Death'. At a somewhat more mundane level were files labelled 'Parliamentary Questions' or ('PQs'). These arose in cases where an MP had raised a question about a Home Office decision. Such PQs would occasionally come my way to look into. I recall an occasion when the same case had led to three! These questions concerned a student whose training was terminated on the ground of inadequate performance (a comparatively rare event).

As I was the inspector who had been given the task of visiting the student to inspect the work and make a judgment, this included lengthy discussion with both the student and fieldwork supervisor. My recommendation that the student's training be terminated was upheld by my superiors. During my stay in the inspectorate I had to deal with two or three similar cases.

The decision to recommend that training be terminated was never an easy one, but one that could not be avoided if standards were to be maintained.

Induction

My own remit as an inspector was to be engaged on training duties. But prior to taking up these specific duties one had to take part in an induction programme into the ways and workings of the Home Office. My fellow appointee (Joan Shepherd: see *Chapter 7*) and I were, with a handful of other recent Home Office appointees, afforded a short but highly informative such programme. I cannot recall now the precise details, but as part of the course we were presented with a problem that required us to draft an appropriate answer to a very disgruntled member of the public. Civility and sensitivity were to be uppermost in our minds, even if we thought the complaint was unjustified. In those far-off days, letters were almost always signed 'I am your obedient servant'. I'm afraid I never regarded myself as anyone's 'obedient servant', and was pleased to note that such designation seems gradually to have fallen into disuse. For all its attachment to formality the department could show a more liberal side. My signature on some letters could be almost indecipherable (it still is!). The Assistant Secretary of State in charge of the division permitted me to use a rubber stamp with my name on it beneath my scrawl. I think she regarded with dismay the likelihood of my signature being read by recipients as Priss, Prious or even (horror of horrors) Piss!

THE TRAINING DEPARTMENT

As I have indicated earlier in this work, I had already had contact with several of my future colleagues, a number of whom were involved in training (and, of course, I had been a product of such training). General oversight of the work of the training inspectors was provided by May Irvine (referred to earlier). She was a very able woman, but was something of a 'workaholic'. It was somewhat demoralising to find that, having cleared one's in-tray on a Friday, it was full to the 'brim' again on arrival, first thing on Monday morning, as a result of her weekend (and occasional Bank Holiday) activity! She could, on the credit side, be supportive of one's endeavours and always took a keen interest in our two children.

At the time I joined the inspectorate the training section was quite small. It consisted of myself, Joan Shepherd, Bob Speirs, Selby Barrett (who had interviewed me some years previously as part of my application to join the Probation Service), and Margaret Hutchinson.

During the next five years our numbers were to be enlarged by the arrival of Mollie Samuels (later Mollie Paul), Peter Westland, Dick Betteridge, Bob Foren, Phyllis Corner, Joan McCarthy and (for a short while) June Mainprice. Colleagues employed on 'outside' inspectorial duties also contributed to the training programme from time-to-time. For example, Ralph Beeson - the deputy principal inspector - came to talk to the students about 'Homes and Hostels' (as they were then called).

In my early days in the inspectorate numbers were small enough for the residential part of the course to be self-contained at Rainer House. However, over time, it became necessary to expand the numbers in training. Rainer House kept its residential element, but teaching eventually took place elsewhere. Some of the courses were quite large and I recall that for a time teaching took place at a curious venue in Whitehall (Palace Chambers).

At that time Margaret Hutchinson organized those courses. Having obtained a degree in mathematics at Oxford University, she developed wonderful algebraic formulae for the organization of small groups. Having failed my [then] School Certificate maths exams, I took fright at her mathematical answers to our problems; when I eventually took over some of her activities, I devised somewhat different methods for dealing with the problem.

My anxieties were fortunately short-lived, because an entirely new departmental venture had come to my aid. The department had decided that what was needed was a larger centre for its probation training activities. They eventually alighted upon premises in Cromwell Road next door to the then Airport Coach Terminal. This was a large building with ample room for fairly large numbers of students for lectures, and it also afforded smaller seminar space. Generous office space was available on the ground floor. There was also a large basement area (which was later to cause major problems). The building required a fair amount of renovation and redecoration. I had recently been promoted to the rank of Inspector Grade I (sounds a bit like grading milk as I said at the time), and with this promotion came the management of the new centre.

I was subsequently joined by Peter Westland and, following Peter's leaving the Home Office, by Dick Betteridge. Dick proved himself to be a most congenial, relaxed and perceptive colleague. Sadly, some years later, a heart condition recurred and he did not survive it. In our labours we were supported by our admirable clerical officer – Miss Hunt.

Although the training inspectors were heavily involved in the teaching at Cromwell Road, much use was made of external staff. We were very fortunate in our ability to attract some excellent psychiatrists to undertake the teaching of both human growth and development and psychiatric aspects of delinquency. Mostly they were senior registrars overseen by the likes of Drs Peter Scott and Trevor Gibbens. Many of these registrars subsequently achieved considerable fame in their chosen specialities. These people included Professor Alwyn Lishman, the neuro-psychiatrist; Professor Griffith Edwards, the drug addiction expert; Professor Michael Gelder, Drs Gavin Tennent, 'Bill' Alchin and Max Glatt, the alcohol addiction expert. Sadly, a number of these excellent colleagues are no longer with us. Various clerks to the justices (such as George Whiteside) taught law.

Some of our graduate students had the advantage of being taught sociological approaches by the late Dr Alan Little from the London School of Economics (LSE). He later became chief research officer at the (then) London County Council. His untimely death, whilst still a young man, was a serious loss. For many years criminology was taught by Professor Eryl Hall Williams, also of the LSE. Members of the Probation Service took seminars in casework. They included the likes of Mark Monger, Joan Sullivan, Doris Sullivan, John Simmons and others. Though I'm probably biased in its favour, the course provided good grounding in the practice of probation and enabled many older entrants to the service to receive training for it. The admixture of younger graduate entrants to the course and these older students seemed to work well.

I mentioned that the building had needed some refurbishment. This certainly applied to the basement, which always seemed damp and somewhat malodorous. It was discovered that there was very serious dry-rot under the flooring. When this was revealed, what greeted us was not much short of something out of a science fiction horror movie! The basement was out of action for quite some time. Fortunately, that part of it that was home to Mr. and Mrs. Brennan, our devoted caretakers, was left pretty well intact.

A ROYAL VISIT

I suppose what could be considered the 'highlight' of my tenure of office at Cromwell Road was a Royal Visit by the Queen and Prince Philip - to formally 'open' the centre some year or so after our occupancy. Of course, I had never been involved in such an event before, and it was certainly an eye-opener! Even in those far-off days, security was a key issue with detailed inspections of the lift and other parts of the building.

There is always the question as to what arrangements needed to be made if Her Majesty wished to 'retire' (readers will understand the meaning of such a euphemism). A suitable toilet had to be allocated; in the event a gents' toilet was found which, with some suitable adaptation (including the name 'gentlemen' being covered over), was made available.

As one of the group accompanying the royal party, I asked our then Assistant Secretary of State (who had overall Home Office responsibility for the event) what I should do if the Queen indicated that she wished to 'retire'. I recall that he replied, 'you accompany her'. I don't think he meant it literally!

After many weeks of preparation the 'great day' arrived. The Queen and Prince Philip were greeted at the main entrance by the deputy chief inspector, Ralph Beeson (sadly Mr. Macrae was in hospital), myself and Sir Philip Allen, then Home Office Permanent Secretary and Alice Bacon, standing in for the Home Secretary.[2] Those who were to be introduced to the royal party were in their correct places (within chalked lines); it all went off quite well, the royal party departing via my office.

It was an interesting, if somewhat anxiety-causing experience for all of us. My recollection of the Queen was of a very well-informed person (she has a reputation for doing her 'homework') and well at ease in such situations. (I have often wondered how she coped with what must sometimes be boring events; I suspect that if one asked her she'd say, 'but that's what I do').

---

2. During some of the time I was at the Home Office Roy (later Lord) Jenkins was Home Secretary. He was a most urbane and well-informed Minister. This was clearly illustrated during an informal meeting we had with him, which had been arranged, as I recall, at his request. I'm afraid I cannot be as enthusiastic about some of his successors, with the notable exceptions of Merlyn Rees (later Lord Rees) and just one or two others who I mention in *Chapter 10*.

One final and slightly amusing comment concerning the visit: there was an extremely large and long window on the staircase leading to the upper rooms. The window was adorned (if that's the word) by very long net curtains. They looked very dusty and uncared for. When I raised the matter I was told the Ministry of Works (as it was then titled) would have them dry cleaned. I knew this would be fatal as they'd fall apart! I discussed the matter with Norma, my wife. Being of a more bold and daring disposition than myself, she said something like 'that's OK, I'll come and fetch them in the car, take them home and launder them'. She did so, with a great expenditure of labour on her part and anxiety on mine! Accompanied by our two small children we brought them back, and somehow managed to re-hang them. Such can be the 'call of duty' for a civil servant and their family members!

MORE TRAINING-RELATED DUTIES

The training inspectors had duties in addition to those outlined above. These included the following: visiting students on their field-work placements in order to assess their progress; visiting some students who had opted to undertake the developing university Applied Social Studies courses under our sponsorship; running short courses for 'tutor' officers who would supervise students on their placements; vetting those main grade probation officers who wished to become senior training officers; and liaising with University Extra-Mural Departments where courses of training had been set up for 'direct entrants' to the Probation Service (mainly mature students). Initially, these were located at Leeds, Leicester and Southampton Universities. On the whole they were successful and a welcome addition to the varieties of training.[3]

---

3. In recent years the arrangements for probation training have changed dramati-

From time-to-time I was 'allowed out' (as I called it) to accompany my non-training colleagues on visits of general inspection. I looked forward to such occasions and learned much from them. The likes of Mr. Morton, Mr. Rocksborough-Smith, Miss Vandy (later) Mrs. Harland and Mr. Beeson all put up with me on a number of occasions.

For the most part I enjoyed my stay in the inspectorate, but I had reservations about staying for a lifetime career as a professional civil servant. I also knew that the time would come when my superiors would consider I needed a move from training to outside inspection. Such a move would involve being out one week and in the next writing up inspection visits. With a wife and two young children, I did not think this was the best way to enjoy marital status and fatherhood.

I had seen a lecturing post advertised at the University of Leeds in the Department of Psychiatry. During my stay in the Home Office my interest in psychiatry in general, and its forensic aspects in particular, continued to attract me. My application for this post and its outcome are described in *Chapter 9*.

---

cally. During Michael Howard's time as Home Secretary, the need for academic as distinct from practical training would appear to have diminished. The specialist Home Office course was closed, and Applied Social Studies courses, as such, also dwindled. A new type of 'training on the job' has been introduced with a major emphasis on 'distance learning' for the academic element. Personally, I'm not at all sure that such a development has been in the best interests of the service.

CHAPTER NINE

Psychiatry and Other Enterprises

Through an error on my part, my initial enquiry concerning the post of lecturer in psychiatric social work found its way to the head of the department of *psychology* - the late Professor Meredith. He kindly forwarded it to Professor Max Hamilton, the Nuffield Professor of *Psychiatry* and head of that department. He arranged for the registry to send an application form to me. All in all, not a very auspicious beginning on my part! A short while after I had submitted my application I was contacted by Marion Whyte, the then current post holder. She informed me that it had been suggested by Professor Hamilton that she pay me a visit for an 'informal discussion' (I suspect that such a visit had been 'engineered' by my future colleague).

Her subsequent short stay with us was a congenial one and any concerns in our minds about a major upheaval were soon dispelled. Marion had approached the normal university retirement age of 65 and the plan had been that I would take over her post. In the event, having spent some years as the sole psychiatric social worker (PSW) in the department, she was so enthusiastic about having a colleague, she persuaded the university to extend her appointment by two years. (To the best of my knowledge, only two other universities facilitated such extensions - Oxford and Cambridge). I was duly called for interview. Unfortunately, this clashed with a date when I would not be available (due to a teaching commitment on the Rainer House course). At this point in time I had not informed my senior colleagues that I had applied for the Leeds post. However, I was due to pay a professional visit to Leeds on another matter, and the university kindly arranged to convene a special interview panel to suit me. The prearranged panel meeting for the other candidates would take place as arranged. I suspect that such an 'accommodation' would be exceptional today. My interview, although quite tough, went well and I was offered the post. (I learned at a later date that I had been Marion's preferred candidate).

My need to move away from the constraints imposed by being a Crown servant, and particularly those imposed by membership of a department such as the Home Office (with all its political 'sensitivities') was an important factor. There were also a variety of other reasons why I thought a move was desirable. As already indicated, it was highly likely that I would be moved from training to 'outside inspection'. The intentions behind such an arrangement were laudable enough - to give inspectors as broad an experience of the inspectorial role as possible.

Futher reasons attracted me to the Leeds post. First, the main element of my work would be to teach and subsequently manage the year's course in psychiatric social work. It was a course with a small annual intake of some dozen or so students. Second, another function of the lecturer would be to work with the medical undergraduates undertaking their four-week attachment ('clerkship') in the department. There was also a limited amount of teaching on the postgraduate course for those doctors undertaking studies for the Diploma in Psychological Medicine (later to become Membership of the Royal College of Psychiatrists (MRCPsych)). There was also opportunity to engage in clinical practice. Third, I had gleaned from other sources that there would be opportunity to develop existing links with colleagues in the areas of criminology and penology. These had been initiated by Marion Whyte (see later).

My impending departure from the inspectorate did not come as much of a surprise to my boss (Mr. Macrae). But, I regret to admit, that it did come as something of a shock to my immediate superior - Miss Irvine. I recall that she blanched visibly when I told her. She felt (perhaps with some justification) that I might have consulted her first. I had deliberately refrained from doing so because I knew she would have tried to talk me out of it or, as she more euphemistically put it, 'talked it through with me'! However, once she had recovered from the shock we remained on friendly terms; and this improved following her retirement from the department. She would occasionally visit Leeds to undertake training events in the extra-mural studies department. When in the inspectorate, she was always a stickler for protocol and formality. She told us during one of her visits that we should in future call her May.

LEEDS . . . AND NEW COLLEAGUES

We made the transition from London to Leeds in good order. Our families took a little while to become accustomed to our removal and our new location in what they regarded as 'distant climes'. My wife's parents regarded Leeds as being 'the back of beyond' (as did many other people I knew at that time). They were agreeably surprised to discover that Leeds is a fine City and the nearby countryside where we had chosen to live was very attractive.

The Department of Psychiatry had a comparatively long history. Professor Henry Dicks, who became a leading figure in the development of marital therapy, had at one time been head of department. Its current high reputation for research into psychiatric and psychological disorders owed much to Max Hamilton. He had been appointed as Nuffield Professor following his work as a Medical Research Council external staff member in the department. His *forte* was really his interest in statistical methods in psychiatry. He had designed and implemented the still well-regarded Hamilton Rating Scale For Depression. Colleagues (some well-disposed to his approach, and some not so enthusiastic) have described him as 'The Max Factor of Psychiatry'!

When he made a brief speech at my retirement party at Leicester (see *Chapter 10*) he said that one of his biggest regrets was that he had never enthused me with his own espousal of statistics in psychiatry - a somewhat embarrassing intervention, and not on the formal speech programme!

Max was unusual in another way. He had read psychology under, as I recall, the late Professor Sir Cyril Burt at University College, London. Readers may recall that after Burt's death it was discovered that he had allegedly doctored some of his research findings in the field of educational psychology. However, such allegations did not extend to his pioneering work on juvenile delinquency (See Prins, 1993). Max was thus entitled to membership (later fellowship) of the British Psychological Society (BPS). I give the body its full title as Max hated the use of abbreviations. He also strongly disapproved of the use by trainee psychiatrists of the 'trade' instead of the medical descriptions of drugs used in psychiatry. His qualification in psychology entitled him to accept appointment as honorary treasurer of the BPS.

There were two 'sides' to Max's character (like most of us). He could be a loyal and supportive colleague - sometimes generous to a fault. He could also be very quick-tempered and abrasive with those who he considered had not come up to his own professional standards. At times such 'outbursts' could be embarrassing, particularly if they were directed to visiting speakers at our weekly departmental seminars. Being a very keen espouser of statistical and evidence-based psychiatry, he was not very enthusiastic towards psycho-analytic approaches in that field. However, he did overcome his prejudices sufficiently to become guardedly sympathetic towards those who did employ such approaches. For example, he was well disposed towards the late doctor Harry Guntrip, the distinguished lay psycho-analyst. Harry contributed to the teaching in the department and also undertook clinical work within it. He had originally been a minister of the church, but had made the cross-over to psycho-analytic psycho-therapy a good many years previously. He had undergone a personal analysis with Dr W. R. D. Fairbairn, an eminent authority on 'object-relations' theory and practice.

Other full-time and part-time members of the department included 'Bill' Anderson as a senior lecturer in psychiatry; he sometimes acted for Max when he was away. Sasi Mahapatra was a young lecturer in psychiatry, who did a great deal of work with the medical undergraduates, and was highly regarded by them. He subsequently developed a considerable interest in the psychiatry of the deaf.

One of our 'external' members of staff was the late Dr Ronald Markillie. He had interests in psycho-analytic group psycho-therapy and assisted us with the selection of students for the PSW course. He was a loyal (if sometimes critical) supporter of our endeavours. Ralph McGuire headed the course in Clinical Psychology alongside Anthony Young. They were joined at a later date by Ullyn Place, a psychologist with a keen interest in philosophy, and by Wilf Hume who, if I remember correctly, had interests in neuro-psychology as applied to psychiatry. Other external contributors to the PSW courses included Mrs. Doreen Collins, who undertook teaching aspects of social administration as applied to psychiatry. She undertook this teaching for several years until it was taken over by Colin Pritchard when he came to the department as second PSW lecturer (see later). Other external lecturers included Dr Leslie Laycock (human growth and development) and Mrs. Maria Farrow (casework). The administrative work of the department was under the oversight of Larry Mullins. I use the term 'oversight' advisedly, because it was clear to some of us that the *control* seemed to reside in the hands of Max's secretary – Joy Brierly!

Max was not deeply interested in delinquency and crime, but was always happy to give support to those of us who were. He told

me on one occasion that, following a somewhat bruising experience as a professional witness in a murder trial, he had vowed
never to become involved voluntarily in such activities again.

The department did have some links with what would now
be called forensic psychiatry. These links were forged mainly with
those medical practitioners who were active in the local prisons.
Two that I recall were Dr Penry-Williams and Dr Alan Weston
(who subsequently went to Canada). These links were also
fostered less directly through the contacts we had developed with
the Prison Service Staff College at Wakefield.

The course in psychiatric social work did not have a particularly happy inception. In those days, such courses (and there
were only a few of them) had to be approved by the Association
of Psychiatric Social Workers (APSW). The Leeds course was
to follow the example set up at Manchester in that university's
Department of Psychiatry. The APSW had serious reservations
concerning the development of such a course in a medical school.
Marion took their reservations seriously and managed to persuade
the department to embrace some of their requirements.

Max had gone so far as to indicate that the department should
run a course without the APSW's approval, and Marion had
offered to resign from the association if approval was eventually not
given. In the event, the course did indeed receive the 'go ahead'.
Marion was not only a good academic, but she was also a quite
determined lady![1] She was an Edinburgh University graduate and,

---

1. The Association of Psychiatric Social Workers (APSW) was a very professional
organization, similar to its sister organization, the Association of Almoners (later
known as medical social workers). In my very early days as a PSW I was asked
to serve on the association's Executive Committee. It used to meet about once a
quarter in quite stylish premises in Park Crescent, Regent's Park. I recall that at
the time I was the only male member of the Committee. I found it initially to be
a somewhat daunting experience to be the lone male representative among those
'doyennes' of psychiatric social work. I guess I gained in confidence as time went
by. During the course of my participation in the work of the association, I met

as I recall, subsequently worked with medical undergraduates at Aberdeen University. She had been one of the tutors to the first dean of our Medical School. On one of Marion's occasional visits to Leicester we managed to arrange that she and 'Bill' Crammond should meet. It was a happy occasion. Marion had travelled quite widely and had held a travelling fellowship in the United States. Among her many wide concerns in mental health matters was her interest in epilepsy; she was a registered 'consul' (as they were then called) for the British Epilepsy Association in the Leeds Region.

While in the United States she had arranged to meet with Professor Lennox, a distinguished figure in the field. She told me with some amusement that when she visited him one of the highlights was the sight of the page proofs of his mammoth two-volume work on the topic laid out on his bed! Marion had a very good 'feel' for words but, to my regret, did very little academic writing. However, we did work very harmoniously together in producing our short book on *Social Work and Medical Practice* (Prins and Whyte, 1972). We had been invited to produce such a book by the late Dr Jack Kahn ('uncle Jack' as he was affec-

---

the other Irvine in my professional life – Elizabeth (Betty) Irvine. She headed up the Advanced Course in Social Casework at the Tavistock Clinic in London. She was also for some time the Editor of the *British Journal of Psychiatric Social Work*. She was well-informed and not a little intimidating on first acquaintance. I still recall her reaction to an article I had submitted for publication in the journal. She turned it down (rightly I think) with the added comment that 'my facility with words would be my downfall'! I hope it hasn't proved to be the case, but the warning has been (and still is) very much with me. Betty introduced my wife and me to Professor Gordon Rose and his wife Jill. Gordon had been seconded from Manchester University to undertake some research for the Department of Health. As they lived nearby we became closely acquainted, particularly my wife and Jill, both having young children. At a later date Gordon and I were to team up with Professor Winifred ('Winny') Cavanagh in providing short courses for newly appointed magistrates (see *Chapter 10*). Sadly, Gordon succumbed to a heart attack - a grievous loss to the academic world. The APSW eventually lost its separate identity with the founding of the British Association of Social Workers.

tionately known). Jack had, I recall, been a medical graduate and post-graduate student at Leeds. He subsequently gained a reputation as a forward-looking community psychiatrist in a London borough. Jack was a well-informed, erudite man. He wrote an insightful book on the illness of Job and its psycho-analytic interpretation. (*Job's Illness*, 1975). We asked Max to write a foreword for our book. He did so in a manner which linked our efforts in a historical commentary on the development of a national health service. At the time of its publication I think it was the first book of its kind.

I was fortunate that Marion had developed harmonious and effective links with colleagues in the field of delinquency and crime. One of these colleagues was the late Dr Harry Edelston – a child psychiatrist who had produced a useful little book on juvenile delinquency. She had also established good contacts with Norman Jepson in the extra mural department. And, as I shall show, I was able to pursue these contacts to great advantage. In addition, good contacts had been established with the Leeds Probation Service, firstly with Alec Bannerman and subsequently with Gerry Bevis. At a later date I used to have regular sessions with him in which we discussed problems and issues of common interest, and particularly those relating to probation.

In its organization the psychiatric social work course was very similar to those already in existence - a mixture of attendance at the university for the academic element of the course and practice placements in some of the local mental hospitals (adult placements at St. James, Leeds, Highroyds and at Menston and Scalebor Park). Child psychiatry placements were mainly at St. James and at local and neighbouring child guidance clinics. Our field-work supervisors were chosen with care. Denis Sharp took the main body of our adult placement students at St.James. (I am not at all sure that he always welcomed our 'liaison' visits to our students with unalloyed joy!).

As was the usual practice, we had regular meetings with our field-work supervisors; from time-to-time, somebody would present a talk on some aspect of social work practice. Our students were a lively and, for the most part, industrious group. One or two of them took up quite interesting posts. For example, Alan Buckley became a senior manager of child care services in, as I recall, Bradford. Nick Hinton, following a spell at Northorpe Hall (see later) gained a senior managerial position in the National Association For the Care and Resettlement of Offenders (Nacro). Both Wenol Hughes and Fionna Kinross married soon after qualifying. Wenol married Paul Blackham, the director of social services for Northampton and very active in professional concerns. Fionna married John Baldwin, later to occupy a chair in Criminology at Birmingham University.

Paul Cheung returned to his native Hong Kong to pursue a career there. Another student (Robina) became the first full-time PSW at the well-known private mental hospital – The Retreat at York. This had been founded by a member of the famous Quaker family of philanthropists – the Tukes. A student with a somewhat unusual background was Nick Stephenson - a member of the well-known Community of the Resurrection at Mirfield. As a postulant, Nick was due to be 'professed' as a monk. He invited Marion and myself to the ceremony.

This entailed an early morning start (I recall well before 5 a.m.) to travel to Mirfield. I found the ceremony somewhat disquieting. It was ritualistic and, if I'm honest, a little 'scary'. The experience resonated for me when I became involved in undergraduate graduation ceremonies in which some of the undergraduates experience a form of 'hooding', akin to a 'laying on of hands'. I'm not sure what Nick's true feelings were about the experience. Anyway, after it he was known as Father Stephenson. The only requirement the course made of him was that on his placements he wore 'civvies'. I recall vividly our children's reaction to his arrival at one of our student parties, when he came dressed in formal clerical attire!

Working with medical undergraduates

As previously mentioned, another aspect of our work was with the medical undergraduates. An important feature of their attachment to the department was a requirement that they 'clerk' (write up) a patient's case history for presentation at the Friday case conferences at St. James Hospital. In order to make such a 'clerking' exercise as comprehensive as possible, the students were required to make a visit to the patient's nearest relatives to complete a personal and social history.

Our task was to accompany them on these visits as 'mentors' and to give support and direction where needed. Most of the homes we visited were in the Leeds area, but occasional visits had to be undertaken further afield. To facilitate the visits, families were always given written notice of our intention to visit. They could opt out if they wished to do so, but very few exercised this option. Visits were almost always paid in the evenings.

I was always impressed by the manner in which our students approached and carried out what could sometimes be a difficult and delicate task. They managed to cope with any apprehension they felt, or at least disguise it once the interview got underway. It may be that our presence helped to give them confidence. Only on very rare occasions did we have to intervene if the student 'dried up'. They also performed well in presenting the case study in its entirety at the Friday afternoon conferences. These were chaired by one of the consultants, most frequently by Sasi Mahapatra. He had a relaxed and warm manner, but not much got past him.

The students' experiences during their attachment were always assessed by them and by us. They almost always expressed satisfaction with the experience and singled out 'the visits' for high commendation. As far as I am aware, this practice of home visiting was only practiced at Leeds. However, when we started the Medical School at Leicester, we incorporated aspects of the Leeds experience into the curriculum. (See *Chapter 10*).

Other tasks and duties

Other duties included occasional sessions with the Diploma in Psychological Medicine (DPM) students and participation in some of the refresher courses for general medical practitioners (I'm not sure how successful these were. I think some of the GPs attended to satisfy professional development criteria and did not really engage with the experience).

I have already referred to the opportunities to develop links between psychiatry, criminology and penology. There were several aspects to these. First of all, and following the lead on the Manchester course, we included a short event on criminal justice and penology. This input was provided by some of the staff from the Prison Service Staff College at Wakefield. The inputs were usually undertaken by David Atkinson (who I was to meet up with subsequently when I served on the Parole Board). He had left the college to work in Prison Department Headquarters. The other college participant was Ian Dunbar. These short sessions proved an invaluable part of the course.

Second, we enhanced the links made earlier by Marion with the extra-mural department, largely through contact with Norman, who eventually became head of the department when his predecessor retired. Norman had a joint post - between the department and acting as senior education adviser to the Staff College. He was an excellent and supportive colleague and became a valued personal friend. He was a modest but well-informed criminologist. I always thought it a great pity that his teaching and organizing duties left him such little time for writing. Another aspect of my contact with the extra-mural department was involvement in training s for magistrates, both new and experienced (see *Chapter 10*).

Third, and a somewhat less direct involvement was membership of what was then known as the Leeds Regional Psychiatric Association. Matters touching upon the links between psychiatry and criminality were often discussed. Fourth, I was appointed to be a member of the Local Review Committee (LRC) of the Parole Board at Armley Prison, Leeds. (The Parole system had been introduced through the Criminal Justice Act, 1967). The LRCs acted in a twofold capacity; first, to provide a mouthpiece for the prisoner applying for parole in addition to his own written representations; second, to assess suitability for parole with the presentation of one's findings at a meeting of the LRC. As readers might imagine, opinions were sometimes sharply divided as to suitability. Subsequent changes in the organization and administration of parole led to the abolition of LRCs.

Fourth, I became involved in the management committee of a local prison after-care hostel.

'YOUTHFUL OFFENDING'

Finally, during my stay at Leeds, a new approach to youthful offending had been introduced within the terms of the Children and Young Persons Act of 1969. This was intermediate treatment (IT). It involved a combination of short-stay residential and community treatment. It was based on the belief that a variety of 'outward bound' activities could halt or prevent youthful criminality. Prior to the 1969 Act, I recall being a member of a small group from the Howard League for Penal Reform who gave evidence to the Advisory Council on the Treatment of Offenders on non-residential treatment for young offenders. Such attempts were, of course, not altogether new. A pioneer in the field was the late Merfyn Turner with his 'Barge Experiment' in north London.

I got to know Merfyn (and his lawyer wife Shirley) well over the years. He was also an important figure in the development of after-care hostels for ex-offenders – Norman Houses. (When we lived in London I had become involved with the Management Committee of a 'Second Norman House'). There were, of course, other pioneer experiments in IT. A former student, and subsequently a great friend, Michael Day (who became chairman of the [then] Commission For Racial Equality and who later became Sir Michael) had established with colleagues motor cycle 'clubs' and work on cars as a means of providing lawful outlets for those youngsters who had become involved in 'twocking' (taking and driving away vehicles without consent). Such schemes proved successful. An IT Centre had been established near the Community of the Resurrection. It was located at Northorpe Hall and provided weekend opportunities for a variety of IT activities. I was asked to serve on its management committee, which proved to be a rewarding experience. It would have been useful to have been able to test its efficacy in keeping youngsters out of trouble had we been able to conduct a trial involving random allocation to the scheme. Unfortunately, ethical considerations outweighed our statistical intent and we had to abandon the idea.

Working with magistrates

During my time at Leeds I had become interested in the extent to which magistrates' courts and juvenile courts (now youth courts) remanded offenders for psychiatric reports. I decided to research the matter at the Leeds and Bradford Courts and subsequently published my findings (Prins, 1975 and 1976). These were much in line with the few other studies that had been carried out, namely that remands were pretty infrequent and seemed to be strongly related to magisterial and probations officers' views about mental disorder and crime. Such matters were discussed in mental health forums, as I discovered during my membership of the regional management committee of the National Association For Mental Health (NAMH), later re-designated MIND. This particular forum included membership from both mental health and criminal justice agencies and I found the opportunities to meet colleagues from both these arenas rewarding.

A VISIT TO THE PALACE

Eventually the time came for Marion to retire. I thought she should receive more recognition than had so far been the case for her sterling work in mental health. On my initiative, the department (with the willing concurrence of the (then) Association of Psychiatric Social Workers) recommended her for an 'honour'. She was duly awarded the OBE. I was pleased to attend the conferring of her award at Buckingham Palace, in company with her brother David. The award not only brought much pleasure to Marion, but to all those who had worked with her over many years.

The ceremony and the surroundings are quite impressive. The 'loos' are a testament to Victorian ornamentation! The only other time I have been to the palace was with my wife to attend one of the regular Garden Parties. If the weather is good it's a pleasant experience and the refreshments are usually excellent!

Following Marion's retirement I was joined by Colin Pritchard. He eventually moved South and was subsequently appointed to a chair in social work at Southampton University. Max Hamilton had been endeavouring to secure a senior lectureship for me for some time, but despite his best efforts had not been successful. I had learned (informally) that I was 'moving up the queue' and it would happen 'eventually'. In the light of this uncertainty we considered a move from Leeds. We did so with very mixed feelings for we had enjoyed our stay and the children had made many friends. The manner in which this relocation occurred is described in *Chapter 10*.

CHAPTER TEN

De Montfort Country

In the autumn of 1971 I received a telephone call from a senior colleague at Leicester University's School of Social Work. He asked if I would consider applying for a senior lectureship in the school. The responsibilities would be two-fold: first, to organize and participate in the teaching of methods of social work practice (otherwise known as social casework), and second, to be involved in organizing and teaching the school's contribution to the recently established Medical School.

LEICESTER UNIVERSITY

The suggestion to apply was attractive, since promotion seemed rather slow in coming at Leeds (despite Max Hamilton's assurances that it would come sooner rather than later). It would also mean that we would be much nearer to our ageing relatives in London, as both sets were becoming increasingly prone to bouts of ill-health. There was also the added advantage of my knowing several of the staff at Leicester. I had had contact with two of them during my period in the Home Office and I had also been an occasional lecturer at the school.

Following serious discussion with my wife Norma, we decided that I should apply, but acknowledged that a move to Leicester might not be terribly popular with our two children! Two of us applied for the post - my friend John Haines and myself. In the event, I was offered the position, I suspect largely because of my experience in teaching undergraduate and post-graduate medical students at Leeds, and a reasonable record of publications.

I had anticipated that John would get the post, given that he was an Oxford graduate and had social work teaching experience at Nottingham University. He was also then a senior training officer with Leicestershire Social Services Department. I think that his formidable background enabled the school's director (Derek Jehu) to persuade the university to create an additional senior lecturer post. So both of us joined the school at about the same time. This event, and the fact that we both experienced a somewhat fraught time (see later), drew us close together, and this proximity has been maintained up to today. My post (which I took up in the summer of 1972) had been vacated by the departure of Miss Priscilla Young on her appointment as the first director of the recently established Central Council for Education and Training in Social Work (CCETSW).

It was only after taking up my appointment that I discovered that a third 'task' had been added to the other two, namely to organize the mental health teaching in the school. The lecturer who had previously dealt with this had been appointed to the Social Services Inspectorate in the Department of Health. On reflection, it may be that my enthusiasm for 'pastures new' had blinded me somewhat to the extent of my future workload.

By the time I took up my appointment the school had been in existence since 1966. It had been established largely on the initiative of the [then] Vice-Chancellor - the late Sir Fraser Noble. I thought Fraser Noble had a real feel and high regard for social work. He had been involved over the years on government committees concerned with both child care and probation. He combined much knowledge with an easy and approachable manner. The school was a unique institution in that it had its own Faculty Board, unlike nearly all other courses providing social work education, which were located in existing departments, such as Social Studies and, as at Leeds and Manchester, Departments of Psychiatry.

As already indicated, its founding director was Derek Jehu (later awarded a personal chair). Derek had trained in social work (child care) and also had a first-class honours degree in psychology – a formidable combination. He ran the school with what I can best describe as a 'hands-off' and benevolent degree of well-informed control. He was extremely popular, and staff were always anxious to do their very best for him. It came as something of a shock when, in 1976, he was appointed to a psychology chair in Canada. His departure left a very considerable gap in the school's hierarchy and management and, as with many institutions that are left bereft of wise leadership, things can deteriorate and undesirable outcomes follow. I elaborate on these matters later in this chapter.

THE SCHOOL OF SOCIAL WORK

At its foundation, the school brought together the courses that had been running in the departments of Adult Education and sociology. The former department provided a non-graduate course in probation work and was sponsored by the Home Office (see *Chapter 8*). The Department of Sociology provided a graduate course in Applied Social Studies.

At the time of my arrival the school provided three courses - a one-year course for graduates with 'relevant degrees' (such as social studies), a two-year course for graduates in non-relevant subjects, and a two-year course for non-graduates.

The quite large intake of students was in sharp contrast to the small number of psychiatric social work students at Leeds (usually about twelve a year). The overall teaching ethos of the school was that a 'generic' approach to teaching could be maintained by making special provision (a form of 'streaming') for students entering a range of social work practice (such as local authority social work and probation). In my view, this was not always entirely successful; it seemed to be based on the erroneous assumption that social workers could be all things to all people.

From its inception the school had been able to employ its own specialist teaching staff, such as sociologists, psychologists and those with academic and practice backgrounds in the various branches of social work (such as probation, social services and medical and mental health social work). To support these internal resources, the school engaged external assistance from within and outside the university. In respect of the latter, psychiatry was taught initially by local consultant psychiatrists (later by staff of the newly established academic Department of Psychiatry). Other contributions came from the Department of Adult Education (ethical issues) and the Law Department. With large student numbers and their diverse needs, a great deal of time needed to be spent in fitting all the various elements together; not always an easy task. And, as at most inter-disciplinary centres of learning, there were occasional competing claims. (For example this occurred in the conflicting demands upon my time between the Medical School and the School of Social Work – see later).

With the aim of developing good relationships with local agencies, and in the university more generally, the school established a programme of regular evening 'Departmental Lectures'. It eventually fell to my lot to organize these. Suggestions were invited from colleagues, and a balanced programme usually emerged. It was also the task of the organizer to entertain the visiting speaker to dinner before their lecture. I recall vividly that on one occasion our speaker (the late Professor Anthony Clare) had been delayed by British Rail. Instead of my well-planned 'wining and dining' in the university's excellent restaurant, a 'pint and a pie' had to be consumed at a pub near the station! Fortunately, such delays were rare and our speakers' reputations were more than upheld by their presentations. At a later date, when I assumed responsibility for directing the school, I found it necessary (somewhat reluctantly) to hand over the organizing of the lectures to a colleague.

The school's internal governance was in the hands of the 'School Committee'. This was attended by all academic staff and our chief clerk. It also included representatives from local services such as probation and social services. Students' representatives attended what we called 'part A' business. Sub-committees of the School Committee consisted of a Fieldwork Practice Committee, and *ad hoc* committees were appointed as the occasion demanded. On the whole, all our committees resolved problems in a highly democratic fashion, though I cannot deny that, from time to time, serious tensions arose (see later).

As already mentioned, social work education and training had been vested in the CCETSW. We survived their inspections, but the work involved in preparing for these 'visitations' was quite considerable, and the task was placed in the hands of a senior colleague with the support of a small sub-committee. I recall that, during the early days I worked at the school, a degree of 'political correctness' held considerable sway, and not always in a sensible and workable fashion. This had its impact on a certain diminishment of teaching in such subjects as law for example. Psychiatry also came in for opprobrium. This was usually led by some of our less well-informed students and, I regret to say, seemed sometimes to be encouraged by certain members of staff. Such subversive activity seemed to me not to be in accord with objective academic debate and discussion.

A NEW MEDICAL SCHOOL

Earlier in this chapter I referred to the founding of a Medical School at Leicester. This was the third new such school to have been established in recent years; the other two being Southampton and Nottingham. The decision to provide a Medical School at Leicester was a significant one. Some aspects of the medical services in the area had apparently not been considered to be of a very high quality, and it was thought that the development of a medical school would encourage and support improvements in research and practice.

One significant aspect of the new school's academic content was the involvement of the social and allied sciences during the first two years of the medical curriculum. The 'Man in Society' (as it was then called) was to be provided by the joint efforts of the Departments of Psychology, Sociology, School of Social Work and the Departments of Community Medicine and Psychiatry. For some time I acted as the co-ordinator of a small group charged with the implementation of the programme. This task was quite onerous and also time-consuming. Fortunately, the convenorship rotated fairly regularly.

From the outset those responsible for the overall design and implementation of the medical curriculum were anxious that candidates should, where possible, have a broadly-based interest in medicine. For example, candidates who had good A-level results in a science subject such as chemistry (a compulsory admission requirement) received favourable consideration if they had also obtained an A-level in a humanities subject such as history or literature. In earnest of this, some of us, in the early days of the school, were asked to assist with the initial screening of candidates' applications. This broad-based approach was fostered by the school's first dean of medicine, the late Professor 'Bill' Cramond (a psychiatrist). He came to us from a high level post in the Scottish Home and Health Department. Bill's enthusiasm for this broad approach was strongly supported in its implementation by the occupants of the Foundation Chairs in Psychiatry (the late Professor Sydney Brandon), and Community Medicine (Professor Marshall Marinker). Sometimes, Bill's enthusiasm for the development of the school had its downside. Evan Bumford (then the school's registrar) would tell us about Bill's preferences for early starts in their travels to see how things were done at some of the more recent medical schools; five in the morning was not unknown, nor was Bill's penchant for fast driving in his small but powerful sports car!

Our first intake of some forty-eight students must have been some of the most carefully nurtured (and monitored) ever to grace a medical school. I recall that one or two of them went on to become consultant psychiatrists; one of them, Penelope Campling, continues to do pioneering work in Leicester in the development of therapeutic community approaches to personality and similar disorders.

Another outstanding student was Nilesh Samani, now Professor of Cardiology at the Regional Cardio-Thoracic Centre at Glenfield Hospital, Leicester. One innovative and practical aspect of the 'Man in the Society' course was the provision of carefully arranged visits to a variety of social service and other agencies. These included visits to social service offices, the probation service, the local prison and a range of voluntary agencies (such as the local Family Service Unit, Society for the Care of the Blind and so on). Having paid their visits, the students were required to attend a tutor-led seminar where they would share their experiences. This innovation proved to be popular.

A further innovation was the attachment of a student to a family having a recently born child. The aim, with familial consent, was for the student to follow up the infant's development for the first one or two years. All of these were very laudable aims and objectives. However, the 'academic path' was not always a smooth one. Quite early on in the development of the school a serious 'dispute' arose concerning a divergence of views about the delivery and content of the sociological input to the course. The concern was spearheaded by the head of psychiatry (Sydney Brandon). The matter was taken very seriously by the Board of the Faculty of Medicine (of which I was a foundation member) and it set up a small sub-committee to look into the matter. As I recall, the Committee consisted of the professorial head of the Department of Law (chair), a senior professor from the School of Education, and the then dean of the Medical School (Professor Sir Robert Kilpatrick, later Lord Kilpatrick).

The school's contribution to the teaching was not in any way in question, but I was asked to discuss with the committee why things may have gone somewhat wrong. I tried to do this in as tactful a way as possible. The matter was eventually resolved, but I think some degree of ill-feeling lingered for a time. For my part, I enjoyed my involvement in the work of the Medical School and found my relationships with the 'medics' congenial, especially those from psychiatry, community medicine, anatomy and physiology. The only problem that arose from time to time was having to serve two masters – the School of Social Work, and the Medical School. On reflection, I think I allowed myself to take on rather too much and it was only when I became director of the school that I gave up direct involvement in the Medical School.

SOME OTHER UNIVERSITY-BASED ACTIVITIES

Within the wider university I became involved in two other teaching activities, both under the auspices of the Department of Adult Education. The first was involvement with another colleague in the school (Kathleen Curnock) in lecturing on training courses for newly appointed magistrates. I recall that one or two of these trainees held very powerful views on the question of punishment. One female course member strongly and very vocally espoused the death penalty. When asked if she would be willing to hold the office of Public Hangman she expressed great willingness! I gathered subsequently that this view and others, no less Draconian, resulted in the non-confirmation of her appointment.

Stereotypical attitudes were not uncommon amongst the

trainees. For example, they tended to see sociologists as long-haired 'scruffs'. My colleague David Webb, an excellent sociologist, and I used to sometimes share a Saturday morning session dealing with sociological and psychological aspects of criminality. One day we decided to reverse physical appearances. David came as a model of sartorial elegance and I arrived in my gardening clothes! These reverse physical appearances may have challenged a few stereotypes.

The second involvement was establishing an evening course for local criminal justice and forensic mental health personnel on Mentally Disordered Offenders. Initially, I ran this course on my own, but on his arrival as the first forensic psychiatrist in the area - Dr Jim Earp - he willingly agreed to join me in this activity. The course proved to be very successful and ran for some years. Jim was the first director of the recently established Regional Secure Unit in Leicester. It was second only in size to the well-established Reaside Clinic at Rubery, Birmingham. This had been a pioneering venture by my friend Professor 'Bob' Bluglass.

As a senior member of the university staff, I was occasionally involved as a member of appointing committees for our own staff and candidates in other departments. I always found this an interesting and revealing experience. For example, a candidate's academic brilliance (say a 'starred' first at Cambridge) would attract almost universal acclaim. However, this needed to be set against strong 'hints' in referees' reports about certain defects in personality, such as arrogance and 'prickliness'. On occasion, I found it necessary to ask how well my colleagues thought the candidate would 'fit' into the team. Sometimes my words were heeded, sometimes not!

SOME EXTERNAL ACTIVITIES

The university recognized that staff would need to engage in a certain degree of 'outside' activity, mainly to enhance relationships with local and national agencies and organizations. In *Chapter 9* I referred to my membership of the Local Review Committee (LRC) of the Parole Board at HM Prison Armley. Following my appointment to Leicester I was permitted to transfer my LRC involvement to HM Prison Ashwell - a then low security (Category C) prison. I continued with this work until I was appointed to the Parole Board for three years in 1978.

In 1976, I was appointed to the Mental Health Review Tribunal (MHRT) as a lay member for the (then) Trent Health Region, until reaching the (then) retiring age of 72 in 2001. Both of these bodies provided me with valuable experience in the area of risk assessment and risk management; areas of interest that still pre-occupy me.

In those bygone days the selection process for such posts could best be described as 'informal'. Concerning the MHRT, my name had been put forward by the Northern Regional Office of the mental health charity, the National Association for Mental Health (MIND). I was never interviewed and I do not recall having to provide any references. I was appointed by the (former) Lord Chancellor's Department, initially for a period of three years, then renewable at three-yearly intervals.

In 1993 I was asked by the Regional Tribunal Office to chair a small, but nationally representative, committee to organize training events for new and recently appointed tribunal members. I continued to do this for a number of years. Appointment to the Parole Board was only marginally more formal. I remember, somewhat to my surprise, receiving a personal letter from the then Home Secretary, Merlyn Rees, indicating that he needed to appoint a further criminologist member to the board. In the knowledge that the workload was a heavy one, I consulted with the vice-chancellor who encouraged me to accept the appointment; and the proposal was subsequently confirmed by the relevant university board.

Having accepted the invitation, I received a letter from the then chairman of the board - Sir Louis Petch - suggesting I have lunch at his club with himself and the board's secretary - Henry Gonsalves; a pleasant enough event, the main purpose being to acquaint me informally with the workings of the board. From the board's inception, a keynote element had been one of informality (as far as I'm aware it still is). The pattern had been laid down by the board's first chairman, Lord Hunt (of Everest fame). Members were known by their first names, the idea being to cultivate a state of *primus inter pares*. I think this innovation *may* have come initially as something of a shock to the system for some members of the senior judiciary. However, during my own time on the board I did not detect the remotest discomfort on their part. Today, appointments to such public bodies as the MHRT and the Parole Board have become much more formal. Posts are advertised, references asked for, and formal interviews held. This more rigorous system helps to avoid suggestions of nepotism. I do not know whether it actually improves the quality of subsequent performance in comparison with earlier less formal procedure. Both bodies have increased in size - the Parole Board most notably so. When I served it consisted of about forty members; now there are some hundred or so. The administrative arrangements have become more complex as a result of this increase, and a wider range of duties are expected of members (such as interviews with certain classes of applicants for parole). The MHRT has also undergone changes, notably in organization and the transfer of central government oversight from the Department of Health to the Ministry of Justice. This latter change had, for a long time, been seen as desirable, I think, by most MHRT members.

My membership of both the MHRT and the Parole Board continued what had been for some time an interest in the assessment and management of risk in criminal justice and psychiatry. Having published several papers on the topic, I found myself involved increasingly in running workshops for a variety of services, most notably the Probation Service. Initial involvement came from what was then the Regional Probation Staff Development Office for the North-East.

My chief collaborator was George Best (no, not the late lamented soccer player!), who had assistant chief probation officer status in the organization. Over the years he proved a most efficient and congenial colleague. These early courses lasted two to three days, were residential and located in hotels offering both comfort and resources. Over the years, various members of the service assisted our endeavours and were excellent colleagues. These early courses in the North-East became known in other parts of the country and, in my so-called retirement (see *Chapter 11*) I travelled widely and spent a good deal of time driving up and down motorways. The probation area making the most regular use of these workshops appeared to be the Inner London Probation Service, working in conjunction with Criminal Justice Associates, an organization devoted to providing a wide range of staff development courses.

AN UNHAPPY EPISODE

When the director of the school - Derek Jehu - left in 1976 to take up a professorial post in psychology in Winnipeg, it came as a shock to the staff. I think that increasing budgetary constraints had become a source of worry and irritation to him and, after some years of excellent developmental work for the school, he felt he should move on. The question of a 'succession' to the directorship and chair became an important matter. A year or two earlier

Derek had given me the clear impression that, if he moved on, he would like me to consider applying for the post. However, he felt that my 'non-graduate status' might hinder me in any application I might make. He consulted with the [then] vice chancellor, Sir Fraser Noble, who informed him that there was a university statute allowing the award of an 'ex-officio' degree in such circumstances. He had never seen it used and considered that my situation would be an excellent opportunity to exercise it! Formal application would need to be made by the Board of Social Work on the basis of a c.v. and at least three nominees, two of whom should be from persons of senior status external to the University.

At a meeting of the board (from which I absented myself at the appropriate time) it was agreed to support such a proposal. In due course, senate awarded me the degree of M.Phil on the basis of the referees' reports and on my record of publications.

I and a senior lecturer colleague, and my good friend John Haines, had let it be known that we were contemplating applying for the directorship. We therefore played no part in a specially convened school meeting to consider views about the qualities needed by possible candidates. Somewhat to our surprise, they let it be known through their spokesperson that they did not feel able to support us. No reasons were given and the senior colleague who had been nominated as their spokesman declined to afford us any. To make matters worse, some few days later, he came to each of us suggesting that, as we perhaps were not like to apply in view of what the colleagues had decided, we might like to join the group to consider who might be suitable!

Tact was never his strong point! We both declined. The following weeks were understandably not particularly harmonious; they were, in fact, quite stressful. On reflection, I think that some colleagues resented the fact that, in my case, the conferment of the 'ex-officio' degree could be taken as pre-judging the outcome after Derek had left. There is little doubt in my mind that colleagues had acted very insensitively in the matter. At the time they were unaware that a small group of senior staff from the wider university, charged with selecting a successor, had deputed one of their number to sound me out to see if I would reconsider my decision not to apply. I gently, but firmly, declined on the basis that running a fairly large department was a difficult task enough; to do so in the knowledge that one's colleagues had, as far as I could tell, reached unanimous agreement not to support an application would make the task that much more difficult.

In the event, out of a strong list of external candidates, an internal appointment was made from within the school. He had an excellent 'track record' in research, largely in child psychology. He did not have social work qualifications or experience. In the light of later events, this may have made difficulties for him. As time went by, he found that the management of a large school was not his *forte* and he returned to the department from which he had come to the school.[1]

The school was subsequently forced into making a further choice. The university had indicated that they were not intending at that stage to make a further external professorial appointment, but wished merely to appoint a director. This time around colleagues expressed a change of attitude in that they agreed that I should direct the school.

Thus for my last three years at the School of Social Work I was its director. Some colleagues, perhaps in recognition that they had made an error of judgement previously, wanted me to apply for a *Personal Chair*. I took their suggestion to the vice-chancellor,

---

1. Because the whole episode was personally upsetting and distasteful, I have not referred to staff by name in this context. Their tactless spokesperson is now deceased, sadly. At a later date, my friend and co-potential candidate, John Haines, left the school and pursued a very distinguished career, first as a social work advisor with CCETSW, and subsequently in the Home Office Probation Inspectorate, retiring as deputy chief inspector in 1995.

who suggested that I should not pursue the matter further. Morris Shock was, in many respects, an excellent vice-chancellor. He combined firm resolve with considerable charm. I always told people that he was the kind of chap who, in sentencing you to death, would make you feel quite good about it! (Maurice if, by any chance, you should ever read these lines in your retirement, you will know what I mean).[2]

Thinking back to those unhappy events, I suspect that some of my colleagues might have considered that I would have found the directorship too much of a strain. Maybe they were correct, for in early 1981 I succumbed to two quite serious heart attacks in quick succession and was off work for a good many weeks. I learned a number of lessons from this experience.

First, the experience of being in intensive coronary care was not a particularly pleasant one.

Second, advice to abandon a life-long habit of pipe-smoking was accepted very readily.

Third, never tell a colleague rather smugly that you had never taken a day's sick leave in ten years, only to find within two weeks of making such a self-satisfied statement that you are in intensive care being punctured and invaded by various pieces of tubular equipment!

TIME TO MOVE ON . . .

Running the school in days of increasing financial stringency was not easy, but we coped. And colleagues were, in the main, co-operative. However, two of my close colleagues, Mary Barker and Kathleen Curnock, had taken early retirement; an opportunity funded in those days by the University Grants Commission

2. Following retirement, Sir Maurice Shock returned to Oxford, becoming the Master of Lincoln College, Oxford.

(UGC). They persuaded me to do likewise. The terms were quite favourable and so, in 1984, I left full-time employment in the university. Following my retirement, Professor Noel Timms was appointed to the directorship and chair. When, after a comparatively short time, he left the school it was headed by a variety of successors, professorial and non-professorial. Some of my activities following retirement are indicated in my final *Chapter*.[3]

---

3. Professorial appointment eluded me when in full-time employment at Leicester. Fate was kinder to me in retirement. I have held professorial appointments at Nottingham Trent University (Visiting Professor for some years), and some time as Honorary Professor in the School of Psychology at Birmingham University. I have been External Professor in Criminology in the Department of Social Sciences at Loughborough for getting on for twenty years, and I currently hold an Honorary Chair in the Department of Criminology at Leicester. Perhaps Leicester could be said to eventually have had second thoughts, or I am just a 'late developer'!

CHAPTER ELEVEN

Not (Quite) Past My 'Sell-By' Date

Early retirement from full-time university teaching did not entail complete cessation of useful employment. As indicated in *Chapter 10,* a number of other activities followed me into so-called retirement. In fact, my wife Norma used to say that in retirement she saw less of me than when I worked full-time! There were various new activities to ensure that I still had a considerable workload.

In 1985 I was appointed to the (then) Mental Health Act Commission (now incorporated into the Care Quality Commission). The Mental Health Act Commission had been established as a result of the implementation of the Mental Health Act 1983. One of its principal functions was to deal with complaints from detained patients. It also had other responsibilities such as the publication of a biennial report on its activities, the scrutiny and approval of certain prescribed treatments of a physical nature, such as psychosurgery and electro-convulsive therapy (ECT), and oversight of the appointment and training of Second Opinion Appointed Doctors (SOADS).

During my term of office the commission was divided into three regions, South, North-East and North-West. I was initially attached to the Southern Region; this covered a huge area and included London, the whole of the south-east and Broadmoor Hospital. Such coverage involved a great deal of travelling, which I found not a little irksome. I asked eventually to be transferred to the North-East Region, which was much more accessible from my Leicester home. The request was granted. I then found myself covering Rampton Hospital, an institution I was well acquainted with through my tribunal work. As with the Parole Board, the commission increased its membership over the years. Sometimes very fine judgments had to be made concerning the validity of a patient's complaint. From time-to-time (and certainly in the commission's early days) our visits were not entirely welcome. I think some staff felt threatened and some degree of hostility seemed never far from the surface. Fortunately, I had experience of 'inspection' work through my period in the Probation Inspectorate. I learned from that experience and from contacts with one or two former HM Inspectors of Education that inspection was facilitated by the use of a 'light touch'.

There is certainly no place for the over-zealous as I think one or two of our colleagues found out. As with all such organizations, there were occasional tensions. However, over the years things seemed to settle down and services certainly did seem to improve as a result of our efforts. However, I was beginning to find the travelling rather too onerous, so that when the time came for my original term of appointment to be extended I decided to call it a day.

NATIONAL CONFERENCES

During this period I became involved in the planning and subsequent chairing of two 'Cropwood' Conferences at Cambridge University. These were concerned with a range of issues involved in the management of mentally disordered offenders. They occurred at a time when central government was planning to encourage diversion of such individuals from the criminal justice and penal systems. I recall that both conferences involved a good deal of careful planning and, to put it bluntly, they were quite 'high-powered' affairs.

In planning these enterprises I had the very valuable support and participation of two colleagues, Mrs. Wendy Start, JP and my friend, forensic psychiatrist Adrian Grounds (from the Cambridge Institute of Criminology and the Department of Psychiatry). But for their input I don't think the conferences would have been as highly successful as turned out to be the case.

In another arena I became involved in the planning and chairing of several large Regional Conferences concerning the provision of services for mentally disordered offenders. These were implemented under the auspices of the Mental Health Foundation. From the small pool of chairmen and women, I recall particularly Sir William ('Bill') Utting - former chief inspector of Social Services at the Department of Health and Social Services, and David Faulkner CB, sometime senior civil servant in the Home Office and subsequently a fellow at the Oxford University Centre For Criminological Research. I think the three of us found chairing these events hard work. For, unlike the small-scale Cropwood Conferences, the Mental Health Foundation events were attended sometimes by a hundred or more delegates.

THE ERA OF INQUIRIES

Inquiries into matters of social, psychiatric and criminological concern are not new. However, it would appear that the past three decades or so have witnessed a rapid increase in the number of these, particularly those into mental health. No doubt our current media-fuelled obsession with risk and public protection has contributed to this. In 1994, a central government instruction made it mandatory to institute an independent inquiry into instances where homicides had been committed by individuals known to the mental health and allied services. This earlier instruction has now been updated and clarified by an amending circular (see Prins, 2007 for details). Personal involvement (as chairman) in three mental health inquiries - two involving deaths - has led me to question whether the proliferation of such inquiries has actually led to improvements in practice.

At the time of writing, I am informed that since 1994 there have been at least some 400 such inquiries (Michael Howlett, Director of the Zito Trust, *Personal Communication* January 5, 2009). Recent inquiries into homicides have, as a recurring theme, failures in communication between services, despite complex structures being in place to secure co-operation as, for example, in the Multi-Agency Public Protection Arrangements (MAPPAs). One may also ask whose best interests are being served by inquiries? Are they set up to establish the truth (a legalistic view), to apportion blame, to satisfy relatives of the victims and of the perpetrators, and/or to recommend reforms? Much has been written about the impact on victims' families and on those being scrutinised, but rather less about those who constitute the inquiry team - particularly those who chair them. I have dealt with this last aspect at some length elsewhere (see Prins, 2004a and b).

An important question for the future must be: are inquiries as presently constituted the most useful way of dealing with such matters? Would, as some commentators have suggested, rigorous internal audit be the most sensible course of action? Of course, it may be the case that on rare occasions a major external (and perhaps public) inquiry will be necessary.

SOME OTHER MATTERS

For a number of years, the two professorial posts I currently hold at Loughborough and Leicester Universities have enabled me to engage with post-graduate criminology students. I teach two similar ten-week modules on clinical criminology. The students are, almost without exception, keen, industrious and extremely likeable. Some of their dissertations on my subject area have been of high quality and a few of them, with my support, achieved publication in professional journals.

In recent years I have, on a number of occasions, suggested to my 'bosses' that I should perhaps give up my teaching, before I overhear the following conversation: 'Nice old chap, if a bit eccentric, but maybe now past his sell-by date!' My superiors appear to think otherwise.

Students sometimes ask me what I consider to be the most significant events and/or enactments I have witnessed in the past fifty plus years of my involvement.[1] I have already alluded to the pioneering Criminal Justice Act, 1948. Alongside this I would recall the Children Act 1948 with its provisions for better care of orphaned and other disadvantaged children (see *Chapter 1*, Note 2). The other statutory landmarks that occur to me are the Homicide Act 1957, the Mental Health legislation of 1959, 1983, 1995 and now 2007. A number of enactments in the 1960s stand out, including the abolition of attempted suicide as a criminal offence by the Suicide Act 1961. The Murder (Abolition of the Death Penalty) Act 1965, was also a quite significant move, as was the Sexual Offences Act 1967 in decriminalising some acts of consenting adult male homosexuality in private.[2]

---

1. Students also ask me what areas of reading in addition to the 'technical' literature might be helpful in their studies in clinical criminology. Somewhat to their surprise, and occasionally to their amused scepticism, I suggest the Bible and some of the great literary giants such as Shakespeare and his contemporaries. Much of my early inspiration for these sources came from my friendship with the late doctor Murray Cox, visiting psychiatrist and psychotherapist at Broadmoor for many years. One of his many contributions to this field, *Shakespeare Comes to Broadmoor* (1992), is a fine example of his approach. See also Professor Russell Davis' book *Scenes of Madness* (1992) and Prins (2001). Professor Femi Oyebode has provided us with a more recent source of learning in his edited volume *Mindreadings: Literature and Psychiatry* (2009).

2. The background leading up to the 1967 Act is illustrative of the various elements that came together to bring about changes in the law. In the early 1950's three quite well-known adult males were accused and eventually convicted of a number of consenting sexual offences with a group of young Royal Air Force men. The latter turned Queen's Evidence against the accused parties. All three were sentenced to varying terms of imprisonment. There was a degree of concern about the sentences and, as a society, I think we were becoming slightly less

The Courts Act 1971 brought the administration of criminal justice into the twentieth century, abolishing as it did the ancient division between courts of Assize and Quarter Sessions. I have referred elsewhere in this book to the proliferation of criminal justice legislation in recent years, some of it leading to confusion for even very experienced sentencers and those who have to administer the system. The complicated Criminal Justice Act 2003 seems to be a prime example of this. On a more positive note, the Sexual Offences Act 2003 has helped to clarify and up-date the law relating to a wide range of sexual offences, particularly those relating to children.

CHILDREN AND YOUNG PERSONS

However, despite this advance, the protection and management of children and young persons seems to have been 'shunted' from department to department in recent years. Its current location alongside departments charged with concerns such as education does not seem to me to have been a very productive endeavour. I have always considered that, ever since Departments of Social Services were established in the 1960s, the special needs relating to

homophobic. Prosecutions appeared to be becoming less frequent, unless there were allegations of a degree of coercion or an 'outrage against public decency'. Advice from the government's senior law officers indicated to police forces that more discretion concerning prosecution could be exercised. A few years later the Wolfenden Committee on Homosexuality and Prostitution recommended that the law should be changed, and that the age limit for consent be set at 21. Over the years, this has gradually been lowered to 18, and currently to 16. Perhaps it needs to be remembered that the 1950's witnessed major concern about homosexual behaviour in sensitive arenas as, for example, in the cases of Burgess and Maclean. Peter Wildeblood, one of those accused of the offences with the RAF men, subsequently wrote a balanced account of his experiences in his book *Against the Law*. Wildblood established a successful career in television production, dying in 1999. (Some of the details of the foregoing account have been taken from the Channel 4 drama-documentary *A Very British Sex Scandal*, broadcast on 21 July 2007).

child care have been lost. I wish no disrespect to present members of OFSTED, but I do not see how some of its members, having little or no experience of child care, can be expected to undertake an inspectorial and safeguarding role. (I am aware, of course, that some former Department of Health Social Services Department Inspectors have now become part of OFSTED). Other endeavours have been more successful. Following the 'Bulger' case, and as a result of a European Court of Human Rights decision, arrangements for court hearings of children charged with homicide and other grave offences are now much less formal.

The 'Baby P' and other modern-day cases have revealed a woeful lack of communication between agencies and, sadly, a lamentable failure of these agencies to see what was under their noses and take preventive action. However, we should not be too quick to pillory social services staff, since they work under great pressure, and in some areas are grossly under-staffed. There is little doubt in my mind that some elements of the media (especially the tabloids) behave in an irresponsible manner on these occasions.

SLOW DEMISE OF THE PROBATION SERVICE

I have referred earlier in this book to the steady decline of the morale and activities of the Probation Service as I once knew it. It has been deprived of its involvement in humanitarian but firm intervention in the lives of offenders. It has now become preoccupied (not of its own volition) with payment by results, with excessive form-filling, leaving all too little time for adequate and vital face-to-face work with offenders.

The introduction of the National Offender Management Service (NOMS) has, in my view, deprived the service of its individual identity and it seems to me to be a top-heavy and over-hierarchical organization. The morale of front-line staff is, by all accounts, at a very low ebb, evidenced by the severe under-staffing that was revealed as a result of an inquiry into the horrendous killing of two French university students.

When Michael Howard was Home Secretary, he did not seem to have all that much understanding of the work of the Probation Service. Successive holders of that post have done little, if anything, to change this view; moreover, the Probation Inspectorate has seemed powerless to engender any understanding amongst our political masters and mistresses. Because of this, the service has been subjected to regular and excessive 'tinkering'. Probation Committees were replaced by Probation Boards, now gradually being replaced by Probation Trusts. I had high hopes for change when, at long last, we had a woman Home Secretary, Jacqui Smith. She started well, but seems to have gone into decline after a series of questionable judgments. We must reserve judgment as to whether her replacement (Alan Johnson, Summer 2009) will do any better. In recent years few Home Secretaries seem to have had the stature and ability of some of the previous office holders, such as 'Rab' Butler, Roy Jenkins, Merlyn Rees and Douglas Hurd.

INFORMATION TECHNOLOGY

The use of information technology has been warmly championed in recent years. It has certainly speeded up aspects of the delivery and storage of information in almost every corner of our lives. However, alongside these *desiderata* must be considered some of the 'downsides'. The data held in IT databases needs to be stored safely; sadly the secure storage of highly sensitive data has been jeopardised on far too many occasions by serious ineptitude.

The government's proposals for the introduction and maintenance of our details in huge data banks constitutes a further manifestation of 'Big Brother' and is equally worrying. There are other downsides. All too often we have seen how access to IT can be abused by people who 'stalk' on the net and those who indulge in the serious abuse of children through it. The ready availability of a range of video games and similar activities for young people is highly seductive and engenders passive engagement. Such facilities can be abused by over-busy parents, who see them as a substitute for their own direct involvement in the lives of their children. IT also engenders an over-speedy response in communication. Nonetheless, colleagues tell me that they spend a quite disproportionate amount of their time sifting through their e-mails each day. (I eschew such technical facilities, sometimes to the irritation of those who wish to communicate with me).

Over-speedy responses can stifle thought and discretion. It can be argued that a letter or a telephone call is likely to produce a more rounded and personal view. This book has been drafted initially in long-hand (with a fountain pen) and then further drafted on a somewhat battered electronic typewriter. My good friend Mrs. Janet Kirkwood (see the *Acknowledgements*) then exercises her wizardry on her word processor. I'm well aware that I can be considered something of a 'dinosaur'; indeed our son once told me that had I been in full-time university work ten years ago I would have had to join the 'club'! So be it.

FORENSIC SCIENCES AND FORENSIC MENTAL HEALTH

It would be no exaggeration to state that forensic science and forensic mental health have developed in exponential fashion in the past few decades. For example, developments in forensic science have enhanced the detection of offences such as arson, and the development of DNA-profiling as a result of Professor Sir Alec Jeffereys' pioneering work here at Leicester has been groundbreaking. There has been some recent evidence that collaboration between forensic *scientists* and forensic *psychologists* can be productive in the latters' work in offender-profiling (see, for example Bond and Sheridan, 2007). Although I touched upon some aspects of these developments in *Chapter 3*, I thought it would be useful to emphasise some of them again in this chapter.

In that chapter I referred to the absence of forensic psychiatric services and, in particular, the absence of forensic psychiatrists for consultation on difficult cases. My recollection is that our present services took root in the 1960s, initially on a very small scale. The pace was no doubt accelerated by the findings of the Butler Committee, which were published in their final form in 1975.[3] The gradual development of medium secure units and the improvement in high secure hospital practice took place in the light of inquiries such as that into Rampton Hospital. The 1970s and 1980s saw a quickening of the pace alongside the development of forensic psychological and nursing services.

Certain pieces of legislation aided this process. For example, the Mental Health Act 1959 permitted the imposition of hospital orders with or without restrictions as a sentencing option. Mental Health Review Tribunals, established under the 1959 and 1983 Acts required increasing psychiatric input and, where possible, panel membership by psychiatrists with forensic experience. The introduction of the defence of diminished responsibility under the Homicide Act 1957 provided an increased opportunity for interaction between the disciplines of law and psychiatry; this sometimes occurred in situations of controversy as, for example, in such cases as those of serial killers Peter Sutcliffe and Dennis Nilsen. Sadly, a degree of controversy continues, but the government's acceptance of some of the Law Commission's modern-day proposals for a modest reform of the law of homicide may eventually improve matters. Many of these problems could be resolved if we abolished the mandatory life sentence for murder,

3. Home Office and (the then) Department of Health and Social Security.

as advocated by many informed people but not implemented by successive intransigent Home Secretaries. The Mental Health Act 1983 developed the need for further forensic psychiatric input. For example, it gave tribunals the power to *order* conditional and absolute discharge from restriction orders without reference to the Home Office, as had been the case under the 1959 legislation.

The murderous activities of the poisoner Graham Young led to the setting up of the Butler Committee, and to the smaller scale (but no less important) inquiry into the particular circumstances of Young's discharge and management. That inquiry, under the chairmanship of the late Sir Carl Aarvold, Recorder of London, introduced what was then known as the 'Aarvold Board', later to become known as the Home Secretary's Advisory Board on Restricted Cases. Forensic psychiatric representation on this Board was mandatory (as was such representation on the Parole Board). In more recent times the forensic 'net' has been widened to include the disciplines of forensic psychology and forensic nursing services. The Mental Health Act 2007 takes such 'net widening' further with its amendments to the approved social worker role, enabling the additional opportunity for psychologists and nurses to carry out these functions.

The Mental Health Act 1959 also introduced the somewhat controversial descriptive term 'psychopathic disorder' into England and Wales. The use of the term was continued in the 1983 Act, but experience (some considered bitter) had shown that the condition was frequently regarded as untreatable; the legal coinage was therefore modified and replaced by 'alleviation', which, in a nutshell, means seeking gradual improvement. With the implementation in 2008 of the latest such Act, the specific category of 'psychopathic disorder' has disappeared as a separate entity, being subsumed under the umbrella term mental disorder. However, the problems of assessment and management are likely to remain.

In 1999 a new term arrived on the forensic mental health scene; the politically coined 'dangerous and severe personality disorder', a disorder said to be present in some two thousand of the forensic mental health and criminal justice populations. The three special units that have been set up to assess and manage this population are still in the fairly early stages of development.

Reading between the lines in accounts published so far, there appear to be problems among the professionals involved in the management of this group. This is evident in four papers published in the February 2009 issue of the *Journal of Forensic Psychiatry and Psychology* (Vol. 20(1) pp 120-154). As with all such innovations, success or otherwise must await the passage of time. Some of us were very much against the introduction of this new category, and I still have serious reservations. However, one favourable outcome has been the deployment of financial resources to bear upon these 'hard to like' people. For the more seriously 'disabled' of this population I think that advances in the neurosciences may, in time, come to assist our understanding and management of them. Such advances will of course not obviate our need to engage empathically with such people, and confront our own 'demons'.

The new Act also removes the previous provision for making restriction orders with set time limits. Such orders are now to be indeterminate. For some of us this was a long awaited and very sensible change; risk can be more adequately determined under such an order. Such an innovation is likely to require increased forensic mental health involvement.

The continuing recognition (but not necessarily the funding) of the need for forensic mental health services has occurred in a number of ways. For example, forensic psychiatry (mental health) has achieved faculty status within the Royal College of Psychiatrists, in the sections devoted to forensic and legal psychology within the British Psychological Society, and in the creation of the Association of Forensic Psychiatric Nurses. As previously indicated, the positive work done by probation officers does not seem to have had the recognition it so richly deserves. There has been a quite considerable increase in the forensic-psychiatric literature, examples being the *Journal of Forensic Psychiatry and Psychology, Criminal Behaviour and Mental Health, The Journal of Investigative Psychology and Offender Profiling, The Journal of Mental Health Law, Psychology, Crime and Law, Legal and Criminological Psychology, The International Journal of Forensic Mental Health, The British Journal of Forensic Practice* and, with its broader remit, *Medicine, Science and the Law.* It is hard to keep up with them all! Text-books on forensic mental health have also proliferated; some of these will be found listed under the section on 'Selected Supplementary Reading'.

In recent years, both the written and visual media have also brought the discipline into prominence. The likes of Conan Doyle, Dorothy Sayers, Margery Allingham, Ngaio Marsh and Agatha Christie have now become somewhat eclipsed by writers such as Colin Dexter, Ruth (Baroness) Rendell (AKA Barbara Vine), Baroness Phyllis (PD) James, Val McDermid, Ian Rankin, Minette Walters, Susan Hill, Mo Hayder and Simon Becket in the UK, Patricia Cornwell, Kathy Reichs, Thomas Harris and Tess Gerritsen in the USA, the late Michael Dibdin in Canada, Donna Leon in Italy, and Henning Mankell, Jo Nesbo, Mari Jungstedt and others in Scandinavia.

Television and the cinema have also played an important part in dramatising the work of forensic professionals. Some of my readers may recall one of the first depictions of the work of a forensic scientist in the late 1960s, with the late Marius Goring as the pathologist Dr Hardy; and, of course at a somewhat later date, the ebullient 'Quincey' in the USA. In recent times, in the UK our TV screens have produced some colourful, if not always very accurate, portrayals; examples being 'Cracker', 'Prime

Suspect', 'Trial and Retribution', 'Silent Witness', 'Waking the Dead', 'Wire in the Blood', 'Messiah', and in the USA, 'Crime Scene Investigation', 'Law and Order: Special Victims Unit'. To what extent these quite entertaining fictional representations have actually led to an enhanced understanding of forensic matters by the general public is much less clear. Documentary programmes such as 'Crime Watch UK' seem much more likely to aid the public's understanding; and, in a number of cases, have assisted in the apprehension of serious offenders such as Michael Stone (see Prins, 2007). All in all, I think it can be safely stated that forensic science and forensic mental health have come of age.

SOME FINAL REFLECTIONS

This book contains a diverse, discursive and maybe a somewhat idiosyncratic history. Four elements stand out in my experience of over fifty-five years.

First, the criminal justice and forensic mental health systems have grown substantially in both size and complexity. And, because of these complexities, there has been the danger of 'throwing out the baby with the bathwater'.

Second, and very closely allied to the first, has been the phenomenon of the over-speedy response and the 'knee-jerk' legislative reaction to social problems. We seem to live in an age of proscription and prescription.

Third, there has been an unhelpful introduction of the primacy of economic considerations leading to an ethos of payment by results.

Fourth, our political caretakers seem quite unwilling and unable to learn from the lessons of the past. However, I was some-what reassured recently to see in the London School of Economics (LSE) magazine a short piece on the fact that LSE Professors Paul Rock, David Downes and Tim Newburn had been invited by the government to write an official history of the British Criminal Justice System.[4] I hope that when it is finally published it will be read by all members of the government.

Finally, in a biographical piece about me in the *Journal of Forensic Psychiatry and Psychology* (March 2007, Vol. 18(1)), psychiatrist Christopher Jones opened his contribution as follows:

> It strikes me that throughout your career you have been someone who has crossed the boundaries between different disciplines, different areas of work.

In view of this, an alternative title of this book could have been *Crossing the Boundaries*. Or, perhaps in not quite so complimentary fashion, *Jack of All Trades, Master of None*.

Readers must decide for themselves.

---

4. *LSE Magazine*, Vol. 21(1) p. 131, 2009.

Select Bibliography

Selected supplementary reading

I have provided a brief selection of some of my own writings that amplify the material contained in some chapters. For a more up-to-date account of aspects of the relationship between criminality and mental disorder, I would refer readers to my book *Offenders, Deviants or Patients?: Explorations in Clinical Criminology* (4th Ed.). London: Routledge, 2010. I have also included works by others in later chapters.

CHAPTER THREE

'Probation and Mental Treatment', *Case Conference*, Vol.2(9), 1956.

'Some Observations on Prison Aftercare', *Case Conference*, Vol.3(10), 1957.

'The Probation Officer and the Domestic Courts', *Case Conference*, Vol.4(9), 1958.

'Probation and Aftercare: Some Aspects of Casework', *Howard Journal*, Vol.XII(1), 1970.

CHAPTER NINE

'Supervision As an Aspect of Education For Social Work', *Child Care Review*, Vol.25(3), 1971.

'Survey of the Agencies Dealing With Offenders in a Northern Town', *International Journal of Offender Therapy*, Vol.13(1), 1969.

'Medical Education: The Social Worker's Contribution', *Social Work Today*, Vol.4(4), 1975.

'Social Work and Medical Education', *Social Casework* (USA), Vol.58(9), 1977.

'An "Example of Compulsory Benevolence" – Intermediate Treatment Examined', *Social Work Today*, Vol.3(4), 1972.

CHAPTER TEN

'Mental Health Review Tribunals: Developing Good Practice', *Tribunals*, Vol.3(2), 1996.

'The MHRT and the Restricted Patient', *Psychiatric Bulletin*, Vol.21, 1997.

Will They Do It Again?: Risk Assessment and Management in Criminal Justice and Psychiatry, London: Routledge, 1999.

Additional material

CHAPTER ELEVEN

McMurran, M., Khalifa, N. and Gibbon, S. (2009) *Forensic Mental Health*, Cullompton, Devon: Willan Publishing.

Moss, K. (2009) *Security and Liberty: Restriction By Stealth*, Houndmills, Basingstoke: Palgrave MacMillan.

Soothill, K., Rogers, P. and Dolan, M. (2008) (Eds), *Handbook of Forensic Mental Health*, Collumpton: Devon, Willan Publishing.

Towl, G.T., Farrington, D.P., Crighton, D.A. and Hughes, G. (2008) (Eds), *Dictionary of Forensic Psychology*, Collumpton: Devon, Willan Publishing.

For an up-to-date account of developments in forensic psychiatry see:

Gelder, M.G., Andreason, N.C., Lopez-Ibor, J.J. and Geddes, J.R. (2009) (Eds), *New Oxford Textbook of Psychiatry*, (Second Edition), Oxford: Oxford University Press. (Volume 2, *Chapter 11*).

References

CHAPTER TWO

Prins, H. (1961) 'The Probation Service and the Magistrates' Courts (A Critical Review)', *Criminal Law Review*, 699-707.

Prins, H. (1964) 'Training For Probation Work in England and Wales', *Federal Probation Quarterly*, December 1-7.

Prins, H. (2007) 'Psychoanalysis and Probation Practice: A Brief Additional Perspective on Smith', *Probation Journal: The Journal of Community and Criminal Justice*, 54(2): 175-182.

CHAPTER FIVE

Prins (1959) 'Some Comments on Delinquent Boys and Their Families', *Case Conference*, 6(6): 160-165.

Prins (1961) 'Psychiatric Social Work in a Boys' Remand Home', *British Journal of Criminology* 2: 149-159.

CHAPTER NINE

Kahn, J. (1975) *Job's Illness. Loss, Grief and Integration. A Psychological Interpretation*. Oxford: Pergamon.

Prins, H. (1972) 'An Example of Compulsory Benevolence – Intermediate Treatment Examined', *Social Work Today*, Vol.3(4).

Prins, H. (1975) 'Psychiatric Services and the Magistrates' and Juvenile Courts. An Analysis of the Views of Probation Officers and Magistrates', *British Journal of Criminology*, Vol. 15(4).

Prins, H. (1976) 'Remands For Psychiatric Reports: A Study of the Practice in Magistrates' and Juvenile Courts in a Northern Town', *Medicine, Science and the Law*, Vol.16(2).

Prins, H. (1993) 'Pioneers in Forensic Psychiatry – Sir Cyril Lodovic Burt – Delinquency and Controversy', *Journal of Forensic Psychiatry*, Vol. 4(2).

CHAPTER ELEVEN

Bond J. and Sheridan, L. (2007) 'The Relationship Between the Detection of Acquisitive Crime by Forensic Science and Drug Dependent Offenders', *Journal of Forensic Science*, 52: 1122-1128.

Cox, M. (1992) (Ed), *Shakespeare Comes to Broadmoor: The Performance of Tragedy in a Secure Psychiatric Hospital*, London: Jessica Kingsley.

Cox, M. and Theilgaard, A. (1994) *Shakespeare as Prompter: The Amending Imagination and the Therapeutic Process*, London: Jessica Kingsley.

Russell Davis, D. (1992) *Scenes of Madness: A Psychiatrist At the Theatre*, London: Routledge.

Home Office and Department of Health and Social Security (1975) *Report of the Committee on Mentally Abnormal Offenders*, (Chairman Lord Butler of Saffron Walden), Cmnd. 6244. London: HMSO.

Oyebode, F. (2009) *Mindreadings: Literature and Psychiatry*, London: Royal College of Psychiatrists.

Prins, H. (2001) 'Did Lady Macbeth Have a Mind Diseas'd? (A Medico-Legal Enigma)', *Medicine, Science and the Law*, 41: 129-134.

Prins, H. (2004a) 'Mental Health Inquiries: Views From the Chair', *Journal of Mental Health Law*, 10: 7-15.

Prins, H. (2004b) 'Mental Health Inquiries – Cui Bono?', In: N. Stanley and J. Manthorpe (Eds), *The Age of the Inquiry: Learning and Blaming in Health and Social Care.* (pp 19-38), London: Routledge.

Prins, H. (2007) 'The Michael Stone Inquiry: A Somewhat Different Homicide Inquiry Report', *Journal of Forensic Psychiatry and Psychology*, 18(3): 411-431.

Index

A

A6 murder 56
'Aarvold Board' 131
Aarvold, Sir Carl 131
Abbie (Grandma Abbie) 29
Aberdeen University 97
academics 42
acting corporal 33
administration of justice 39
adoption 48
Adosides, Mrs. 27
adult education 107
'advise, assist and befriend' 41
Advisory Council on the Treatment
    of Offenders 102
after-care 48, 102
Alchin, Dr 'Bill' 86
Allen, Sir Philip 88
'alleviation' 131
Allingham, Majory 133
Alumni Magazine 134
Amalgamated Engineering Union 30
America 38, 41
Ampthill 50, 52, 55
anatomy 112
Anderson, 'Bill' 95
Anderson, Miss 76
anti-semitism 34
anxiety 68
Applied Social Studies courses 89
approved school
    approved school assess-
        ment service 66
    classifying centre 65
approved social worker 131

Arlesey, Bedfordshire 58
Armley Prison, Leeds 102, 114
arrogance 113
Ashwell, HM Prison 114
assessment 131
Assizes 126
Association of Forensic Psychiatric
    Nurses 133
Association of Psychiatric Social
    Workers (former) 96, 104
Astbury, Benjamin 39
Atkinson, David 101
attendance centre 46

B

'Baby P' 127
Bacon, Alice 88
bail 67
Baker, Lancelot 27
Baldwin, John 99
Bannerman, Alec 98
Banquo 23
'Barge Experiment' 102
Barker, Mary 119
Baron, Bernhard 37
Barrett, Selby 40, 85
Basford, Eric 52
Becket, Simon 133
Bedford 45
Bedfordshire 44, 45, 72
Beeson, Ralph 54, 85, 88, 90
behaviour
    prolonged history of dis-
        turbances 67
    understanding behaviour 24
Benson, Sir George 78
Berlin Airlift 33
Bernhard Baron Settlement 37
Best, George 116

Grendon Prison (formerly Grendon
    Underwood) 47
Grounds, Adrian 122
Group G motor-cycle test 34
guardian ad litem 48
Guntrip, Dr Harry 94

H

'habitual criminal' 46
Haines, John 105, 117
Hall Williams, Professor Eryl 87
Halmos, Dr. Paul 39
Hamilton, Professor Max 91, 93,
    104, 105
Hamilton Rating Scale For Depres-
    sion 93
Hanratty, James 50
'hard to like' people 132
Harland, Mrs 90
Harris, Saunders 76
Harris, Thomas 133
Harrow 70, 71
harsh sentencing 57
Hayder, Mo 133
health and safety 53
heart attack 119
Henderson, QC, Charles 57
Hendon Magistrates' Court 70, 72
Henriques, Sir Basil 37
Higgins, Aire Commodore (retired)
    55
Highroyds 98
high secure hospital 130
High Sheriff 57
Hill, Susan 133
Hinton, Nick 99
history, learning from 134
history taking 68
Hitchin 51

Holland 24, 37
Home Counties 65
Home Office 40, 43, 45, 61, 73, 76,
    79, 81, 92, 105, 107, 123,
    131
  'check-list' of tasks (probation) 43
  Home Office Children's
      Department 76
  Home Office Proba-
      tion Course 73
  Home Office Probation In-
      spectorate 40, 48, 54
  induction programme 84
  memos 83
  'unfit for purpose' 81
'Homes and Hostels' 85
Home Secretary 81, 114, 128, 131
Home Secretary's Advisory Board of
    Restricted Cases 131
home surroundings report 47
home visiting (as part of student
    courses) 100
home visits 52
homicide 123, 124
  Homicide Act 1957 125, 130
  law reform 130
homosexual advances 34
homosexuality 44, 125
Hong Kong 99
'hooding' 99
Hornby, Sally 64
horseback 51
hospital orders 130
Howard League for Penal Reform
    78, 102
Howard, Michael 90, 128
Howarth, Elizabeth 62, 77
Howlett, Michael 124
Hughes, Wenol 99
human frailty 57

So You Think You Know Me?
by Allan Weaver

The autobiography of an ex-offender and twice-times inmate of Barlinnie Prison, now a social work team-leader in his native Scotland... 'I thoroughly recommend this book to anyone who wants to be reminded of why they embarked on a career in the probation service': *Probation Journal*

2008 | 224 pages | ISBN 9781904380450

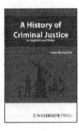

A History of Criminal Justice in England and Wales
by John Hostettler

Charts all the main developments of criminal justice, from Anglo-Saxon dooms to the Common Law, struggles for political, legislative and judicial ascendency and the formation of the modern-day Criminal Justice System ... 'A good book from a well-respected publishing house': *Prison Service Journal* ... 'At a cost of a few gallons of petrol it is a fantastic bargain': *Criminal Law and Justice Weekly*

2009 | 352 pages | ISBN 9781904380511

Sir William Garrow
His Life, Times and Fight for Justice
by John Hostettler and Richard Braby

A gem of a book - a comprehensive account of lawyer William Garrow's life, career, family and connections ... 'Garrow can truely be said to have revolutionised the practice of criminal law': **Geoffrey Robertson QC** (from the *Foreword*) ... 'A blockbuster of a book': **Phillip Taylor MBE**

2009 | 272 pages | ISBN 9781904380559

More details at WatersidePress.co.uk

☷ WATERSIDE PRESS